DATE DUE

NOV 1 9 1996		
JUN 1 8 2009		

HIGHSMITH   #45102

Debrett's

GUIDE TO
HERALDRY
AND REGALIA

The coat of arms of Winthrop Williams Aldrich (1885–1974), United States Ambassador to the Court of St James's from 1953 to 1957. Mr Aldrich was a distinguished lawyer and banker as well as a diplomat and in the course of his long career received many honours, including that of Honorary Knight Grand Cross of the Order of the British Empire which entitled him to supporters. The insignia of the Order are also shown in this fine depiction of the arms he was granted in 1956.

Debrett's
GUIDE TO
HERALDRY
AND REGALIA

FOREWORD BY SIR COLIN COLE, KCVO, TD,
GARTER PRINCIPAL KING OF ARMS

DAVID WILLIAMSON

HEADLINE

For
André

First published in 1992 by
HEADLINE BOOK PUBLISHING PLC

10 9 8 7 6 5 4 3 2 1

British Library Cataloguing in Publication Data
Williamson, David
  Debrett's Guide to Heraldry and Regalia
  I. Title
  929.6094

ISBN 0-7472-0609-0

Printed and bound in Spain by
Artes Graficas Toledo, S.A.
D.L.TO:1165-1992

HEADLINE BOOK PUBLISHING PLC
Headline House
79 Great Titchfield Street
London W1P 7FN

Typesetting by ICON Exeter

CONTENTS

FOREWORD

In the first half of this century books on heraldry and regalia were few in number, of some weight and rather expensive to acquire – especially for the young student – even in the secondhand book market. The post-war period, contrastingly, is remarkable for the increasing demand for such works and the multiplication of those seeking to know more about heraldry, regalia and connected subjects.

To the pleasure and interest that has been acquired from such study there has been added a greater knowledge of the social, civic and public history of this country, and the value of the ceremonies inherent in the functioning of a constitutional monarchy has become more greatly appreciated.

Debrett's has long been a leader in the field of publications on such subjects (its Dictionary of the Coronation (1902) and Debrett's Heraldry (1914) are examples) and now this latest volume is added, a novel coupling of heraldry and regalia, in the form of a guide to both.

As well as covering British heraldry, this book also provides a good measure of useful facts about official heraldic systems from other countries and, taking on an almost universal aspect, relates something of the history of the various rituals of coronation involving the use of regalia and like tokens of recognition before and since the beginning of the Christian era.

In modern times what is endemic in humankind has not been cast aside: identifying insignia of various kinds are much employed and heraldic expression is everywhere to be noticed. Indeed, in some cases these are enjoying a renaissance. To take but one example – distinctive flags, some decked with armorial bearings and like devices, are being displayed as symbols of the independence desired by the Countries of the Baltic and those elsewhere seeking the realization of their nationhood. A symbol enshrines the history of a people; its soul is revealed by traditional colours and emblems.

To study this guide, and its wealth of illustrations, will be an enjoyable and profitable exercise, whatever the level of understanding of the subjects. The records of the past, it was affirmed a hundred years ago by a King of Arms, are a storehouse of culture and delight. The greater such delight must be when it comes from a source that is up to date and accurate as well: and these are the qualities which the author, David Williamson of Debrett's, has striven to bring to this work and for succeeding in which he deserves every commendation.

Sir Colin Cole, KCVO, TD,
Garter Principal King of Arms

INTRODUCTION

In the popular imagination heraldry probably conjures up images of knights in armour with beplumed helmets, brandishing lances and brightly coloured shields – similar to those which are to be found on sale all over London in the cheaper kind of souvenir shop. Mention of a herald, on the other hand, evokes the image of a comical figure in a quasi-medieval costume, surmounted by a squashy black velvet tammy of the kind favoured by Victorian artists and composers, and forever strutting about pompously on spindly legs. He also clutches a large scroll of parchment, which he will unroll from time to time and read from in sonorous tones. It is not unknown for him to blow a trumpet.

Such, then, are the popular images of heraldry and heralds. It is the purpose of the first part of this book to set the record straight and supply a concise, accurate and, it is to be hoped, informative and amusing account of what heraldry is, what it has been, and its application to life today.

The second part of this book deals with regalia. Again, most minds will envisage mayoral or masonic regalia on hearing the word. Only those who have perhaps recently visited the splendid display of British Crown Jewels in the Tower of London and the interesting, though less spectacular, items in the Museum of London, will think of those ancient symbols of royal rank which have been common to almost every nation of the world since the dawn of civilization.

Britain is particularly lucky to possess such a full set of royal regalia with a well-documented history and one, moreover, which is still used, not only at coronations, but annually at the State Opening of Parliament. On this occasion the sovereign still appears in full majesty wearing the Imperial State Crown, in a ceremony whose origins can be traced back to the 'solemn crown wearings' of Britain's medieval kings.

Other countries in Europe also possess sets of regalia of differing degrees of splendour, but sadly in those which have not become republics, coronation ceremonies have long been discontinued and, if their regalia are used at all, it is only to be displayed symbolically at royal weddings or at royal inaugurations or oath-takings. At the wedding of the present King and Queen of Sweden their crowns were displayed at either end of the altar; at her inauguration, the Queen of the Netherlands, although arrayed in an ermine-trimmed royal mantle, had the crown and other regalia displayed on a table before her; and the King of Spain took the oath in the Cortes with the crown (which had been mislaid and was only found just in time for the ceremony) also displayed on a low table.

It is believed that the only other country in the world whose monarchs are still crowned in a Christian ceremony is the Kingdom of Tonga, where King Taufa'ahau Tupou IV was crowned in the Royal Chapel by his Methodist chaplain. Royal regalia also exist in non-Christian countries and coronations of varying magnificence are still held in Thailand (Buddhist), Nepal (Hindu), Malaysia (Muslim), and elsewhere. In Japan the ceremonies attendant upon the enthronement of an emperor are often spoken of as coronations, but since there is no actual crown this is a misnomer.

Non-royal regalia comprise the civic trappings of lord mayors and mayors, of masters and other members of Livery Companies, and the numerous 'jewels', aprons, collars and cuffs employed in their ceremonies by the masonic lodges, and these will be briefly dealt with.

The subjects of heraldry and regalia, although overlapping at several points, have never been covered in one volume before and this attempt to do so may stimulate a new interest in both and lead a few at least to further study. The illustrations have been carefully chosen to enhance the text and form an integral part of the book, while the information given in the appendices is intended to provide a reference tool of lasting value.

DAVID WILLIAMSON

PART 1

Heraldry

The hearse, or temporary funeral monument, designed by Maximilian Colt and erected in
Westminster Abbey to cover the tomb of Anne of Denmark, Queen of James I, in 1619.

CHAPTER 1

The Origins and
Development of Heraldry

Since earliest times tribal groups throughout the world have adopted symbols or totems to distinguish them from other groups and render themselves easily recognizable to each other. Such symbols can be seen in ancient Egyptian and Babylonian paintings and sculptures; in China, where the five-toed dragon early became the symbol of the emperor, with the phoenix that of the empress; and in Japan, where the imperial symbol is the chrysanthemum and a system of family symbols, known as *mons*, has grown in very similar fashion to its counterpart in Western heraldry. The eagle standards of imperial Rome were echoed by those carried by the Aztecs in Mexico, which were to be adopted and adapted by their Spanish conquerors. The totem poles of the North American Indians have their counterpart in the ancient totem animals of early Europe, the white horses, the red dragons, the hares and the black bulls' heads, remnants of which have survived to this day to be incorporated in both public and private arms.

Although emblems such as these soon became common to nations and smaller tribal groupings, many centuries were to pass before a heraldry specific to individuals or families evolved. When it did, it happened with almost amazing suddenness.

At the time of the Norman Conquest, as can be seen from the Bayeux Tapestry, both the English and the Normans carried shields and standards painted with devices of one sort or another, but these appear to have been purely decorative and by no means exclusive to an individual. Furthermore, accounts of the Battle of Hastings relate that a rumour that Duke William had been killed was only countered when he removed his helmet and showed himself to his followers, an expedient which would not have been necessary had he borne a shield with a recognizable device or surmounted his helmet with a recognizable crest.

Sixty years after the Conquest a contemporary account of the marriage of William the Conqueror's granddaughter, the widowed Empress Maud, to Geoffrey, Count of Anjou, informs us that King Henry I knighted his

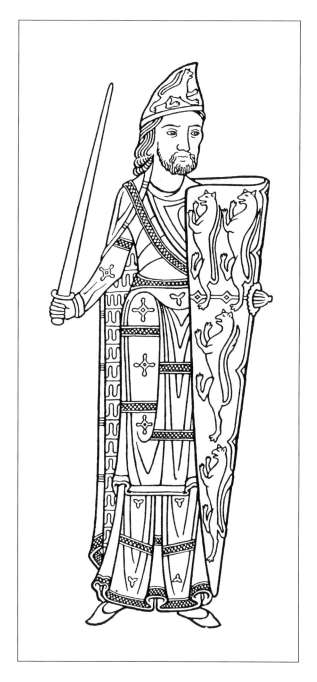

Geoffrey Plantaganet, Count of Anjou. Taken from the
enamel plaque marking his burial place in Le Mans
Cathedral, this drawing shows him with the shield he
received from his father-in-law King Henry I.

new son-in-law and hung around his neck a shield charged with golden 'lioncels'. When Geoffrey died in 1151 his tomb in Le Mans Cathedral was marked by an enamel plaque (now in Le Mans Museum) depicting him bearing this very shield, which covers his body from neck to toe and on which the field is blue and the 'lioncels' (an indeterminate number) are gold. Two generations later the same arms (azure, six lions rampant or, three, two and one) were borne by Geoffrey's grandson, William Longespee, Earl of Salisbury, an illegitimate son of King Henry II, and are to be seen depicted on his tomb in Salisbury Cathedral. This is quoted as the first-known example of true heraldry in western Europe and there can be no doubt that from the late twelfth century onwards the Crusades gave such impetus to the new science that the rules governing its use proliferated.

The kings and nobles who took the cross soon found they had to devise some means whereby they could recognize each other easily when clad in armour and, equally, be recognized by their followers. To this end, we find King Richard I adopting as his cognizance the leopards (later lions) of England, gold on a red field, and the King of France adopting gold lilies on a blue field.

To combat the effect of the heat of the eastern Mediterranean sun on their metal armour, the Crusaders devised white linen surcoats and these, painted also with their heraldic emblems, became the original 'coats of arms'. These were later extended to horse trappings and at the same time it became customary for kings, nobles and knights to have the arms they adopted engraved on their seals. Crests, the modelled three-dimensional devices sometimes (though by no means always) taken from a motif in the arms and attached to the helmet, evolved some time later and only came into general use in the reign of Edward III (1327–1377).

Heraldry soon touched every aspect of upper-class life and was used in profusion, either as a mark of ownership or for pure decoration, on clothes, furniture and wood, stone and metal work, on tombs, houses, churches and vestments – in fact on every artefact of daily life. Stories could be told by heraldry and many pedigrees have been unravelled by the correct identification of coats of arms embellishing medieval tombs.

Once armory (heraldry) had become an established science, the enthusiasm of its practitioners led them to attribute arms not only to the kings preceding Richard I, but even to the biblical patriarchs and mythological personages of ancient times. Thus we find gules, a horse salient argent, attributed to the kings of Kent; azure, three crowns or, to the kings of the East Angles; a saltire to the kings of Mercia; a golden dragon to the kings of Wessex; and so on. Egbert (802–839), is credited with bearing azure, a cross moline argent. A little over a century later King Edgar (959–975) is alleged to have borne azure, a cross flory between four doves or, and a

The tomb of Edmund of Langley, Duke of York (1341–1402), the fifth son of King Edward III. He died at King's Langley, Hertfordshire, and was buried with his first wife Isabel of Castile (*d*1393). Their magnificent tomb of alabaster and Purbeck marble was built before Edmund's death and is decorated on three sides with a series of heraldic shields demonstrating his family connections. Originally in the Church of the Mendicant Friars at King's Langley, it was moved after the Dissolution of the monasteries to the town's parish church, and has been in its present position since 1877.

fifth dove is added to the arms attributed to Edward the Confessor (1042–1066), some of whose silver pennies carry a reverse design of a cross with a bird in each angle, which probably inspired the notion.

The arms attributed to the unfortunate Harold II (1066) are far more elaborate, being blazoned as gules crusily argent, two bars between six leopards' faces, three, two and one. However, the Bayeux Tapestry shows the old dragon standard of Wessex being borne in Harold's army and the dragon as a symbol is certainly of great antiquity in Britain, possibly deriving from a Roman military ensign.

The arms attributed to William the Conqueror (1066–1087) and his sons William Rufus (1087–1100) and Henry I (1100–1135) are gules, two lions (sometimes blazoned as leopards) passant guardant or; while the arms attributed to King Stephen (1135–1154) are blazoned as gules, a sagittarius or (in some versions, gules, three sagittarii or). This is thought to be an allusion to the fact that Stephen ascended the throne when Sagittarius was the sign of the zodiac. It has also been conjectured that it may have been his birth sign, which would render its choice doubly appropriate.

The arms attributed to King Henry II (1154–1189) are the same as those attributed to his Norman predecessors but by the end of the reign the royal arms had become gules, three golden lions passant guardant. These passed on to his successors, including his son Richard I with whom, as we have seen, heraldry proper began, and still form the first and fourth quarterings of the royal arms today.

One of the most important examples still in existence of early heraldry is provided by the seals attached to a letter which was prepared (though never sent) as a reply to a Bull of Pope Boniface VIII in which the Pope claimed the feudal overlordship of Scotland for himself and his successors in the Holy See. The Bull was addressed to King Edward I and was the Pope's response to a petition from the Scots made after their defeat by the English at Falkirk on 22 July 1298. They had asked the Pope to declare that the King of England had no superiority to the King of Scots, but to the rage and dismay of both Scots and English, Boniface seized the opportunity to abrogate the overlordship of Scotland for himself. The Bull, which was dated at Anagni on 27 June 1299, was delivered to Edward by the Archbishop of Canterbury in August 1300 and a Parliament was summoned to be held at Lincoln the following January to consider how the matter should be dealt with. The reply which was drafted and is dated 12 February 1300/1, has the armorial seals of seven earls and ninety-six barons appended thereto. For rather complex political reasons, the letter was never sent to the Pope, but it remains as a splended collection of armorial seals of the English nobility of the day. Most of the seals, which are objects of great beauty, bear a figure of the

PREST·DE·A·COMPLIR

The tomb of Edward, 8th Earl of Shrewsbury (d1618), and his wife Jane
(d1625), daughter of Cuthbert, 7th Lord Ogle. The couple died childless and
were buried under this magnificent tomb in Westminster Abbey which the
heralds of the day faithfully copied into their books. The Earldom passed to a
distant cousin.

This delightful painting of William Longespee, Earl of Salisbury, by the late Gerald Cobb was first published in Harold B Pereira's *The Colour of Chivalry* (1950) and is based on William's monumental effigy. He is depicted in chain mail and his shield and surcoat bear the arms, six gold lions on a blue field, which appeared on the shield given to his grandfather Geoffrey Plantagenet, Count of Anjou, by his father-in-law King Henry I on the occasion of his marriage.

John of Eltham, Earl of Cornwall, was the younger son of King Edward II and Isabel of France and was born at the Royal Manor of Eltham in Kent on 25 August 1316. He was created Earl of Cornwall in 1328 and twice acted as Guardian of the Realm during his brother King Edward III's absences in France. He died unmarried at Perth in Scotland on 13 September 1336 and was buried in Westminster Abbey. This picture by Gerald Cobb is based on his monumental effigy and shows him bearing his heraldic shield of England within a bordure of France.

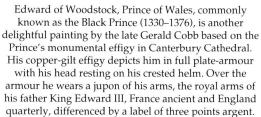

Edward of Woodstock, Prince of Wales, commonly known as the Black Prince (1330–1376), is another delightful painting by the late Gerald Cobb based on the Prince's monumental effigy in Canterbury Cathedral. His copper-gilt effigy depicts him in full plate-armour with his head resting on his crested helm. Over the armour he wears a jupon of his arms, the royal arms of his father King Edward III, France ancient and England quarterly, differenced by a label of three points argent.

Margaret Beauchamp, Countess of Warwick (d1406). Gerald Cobb's painting of this great lady is based on her monumental brass in St Mary's Collegiate Church, Warwick, where she lies beside her husband Thomas Beauchamp, Earl of Warwick (d1400). Margaret was the daughter of William, Lord Ferrers of Groby, and her kirtle is charged with the arms of the Ferrers family, gules, seven mascles, three, three and one, while her mantle bears the Beauchamp arms, gules, a fess between six cross crosslets or. Her little dog gazes up trustingly at her feet.

Above left: A lively representation by Hector le Breton of James III, King of Scots, and his Queen, Margaret of Denmark: hardly good likenesses of the royal couple, but their heraldic garb renders them instantly recognizable.

Above right: The arms of Christ: a typical example of the imaginary arms attributed to historical and mythical characters by medieval heralds.

An early medieval roll of arms.

A section of a roll of arms of 1483 showing the shields, crests and badges of some Yorkshire lords.

owner in full armour on a caparisoned horse on the obverse and a shield of arms on the reverse. In the majority of cases, the colours, or tinctures as they are called in heraldic parlance, can be supplied from the Roll of Caerlaverock, a rhyming summary in French of all those who took part in the siege of Caerlaverock Castle on 11 July 1300.

The rapid growth of heraldry created a need for skilled exponents of the art and the formulation of what today would be called 'a code of practice'. Heralds are found in the households of kings and great nobles some two hundred years or more before the incorporation of the College of Arms. Their development and the history of the College will be dealt with in a later chapter (Chapter 3). In the meantime, explanation is needed of the 'rules' and terminology of heraldry.

CHAPTER 2

The Rules of Heraldry

Coats of arms are usually displayed on a shield, the shape of which can vary. The arms of ladies are shown on a diamond-shaped lozenge or occasionally on an oval cartouche, although the arms of a queen regnant, queen consort, or queen dowager are displayed on a shield like those of a man. A written description of a coat of arms is called a blazon and is couched in heraldic language, which includes many French words. The colours used are known as 'tinctures' and consist of two metals, or (gold) and argent (silver); and eight colours, azure (blue), gules (red), sable (black), vert (green), purpure (purple), tenne (tawny orange), sanguine (blood red) and murrey (mulberry). The last three of these, sometimes referred to as 'stains', are seldom encountered in English heraldry. In addition to the above metals and tinctures there are eight 'furs', ermine (black spots on white), ermines (white spots on black), erminois (black spots on gold), pean (gold spots on black), vair (an arrangement of white and blue pieces, representing the belly and back skins of a squirrel), counter-vair (the opposite of vair), potent (an arrangement of T-shaped pieces in blue and white), and counter-potent (the opposite of potent).

Having learned the tinctures, the student of armory would be well advised to heed the words of that great herald Oswald Barron FSA, whose masterly article on heraldry, written for the *Encyclopaedia Britannica* in 1910, has never been bettered. He wrote:

> An ill-service has been done to the students of armory by those who have pretended that the phrases in which the shields and their charges are described or blazoned must follow arbitrary laws devised by writers of the period of armorial decadence. One of these laws, and a mischievous one, asserts that no tincture should be named a second time in the blazon of one coat. Thus if gules be the hue of the field any charge of that colour must thereafter be styled 'of the first'. Obeying this law the blazoner of a shield of arms elaborately charged may find himself sadly involved among 'of the first', 'of the second', and 'of the third'. It is needless to say that no

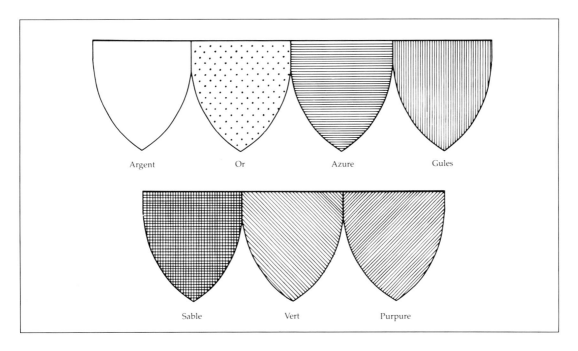

This system of hatching is often used to indicate the colours of a coat of arms depicted in black and white.

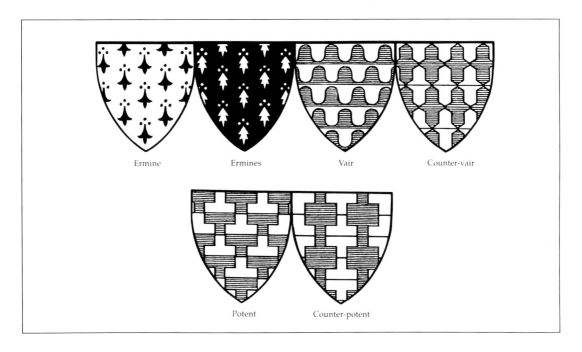

Some of the heraldic furs as represented in black and white.

such law obtained among armorists of the middle ages. The only rule that demands obedience is that the brief description should convey to the reader a true knowledge of the arms described.

The charges (devices) borne on a shield of arms are of almost infinite variety. Apart from designs which appear merely abstract or geometrical, divided and subdivided by eleven varieties of line (for which the reader is advised to consult the Glossary), they can be drawn from the animal, vegetable or mineral kingdoms. Animals, both real and fabulous, have always been a favourite charge and can often be related to an incident in the life of the first to bear those arms or to an alleged exploit of one of his ancestors. Trees, leaves, fruit and flowers are also frequently found charges, being particularly common in examples of 'canting' arms, that is to say arms in which the charge is a pun on the name of the bearer. Thus a family of Perry might bear three pears as a charge, a family of Appleton three apples, a family of Rose three roses, and so on. This form of heraldic joke still survives and a good example occurs in the recently granted arms of Tooke (to be described more fully in Chapter 5), where two keys were chosen, as a play upon the name.

A strict rule of heraldry which must always be observed is that a colour is always placed upon a metal, never upon another colour, and vice versa. The one and only exception to this rule is to be found in the arms of the Crusader Kingdom of Jerusalem, in which five gold crosses are placed on a silver field. This appears to have been done deliberately in order to exalt the arms of the Holy Land above all others.

So far we have dealt with shields, have barely mentioned crests, and said nothing at all about supporters. The crested helm became an adjunct of the shield from a very early period. From ancient times warriors had borne wings, horns or animal heads on their helmets when riding into battle. The purpose of these was probably both to strike fear and terror into the hearts of the enemy and to provide a focal point for the rallying of their own men. Parallel developments may be seen in the grotesque masks and headdresses used in the rituals of many primitive tribes in Africa and elsewhere, and in the fearsome armour of the Japanese *samurai*. Whereas shields by their nature and purpose could only be one dimensional, crests were three dimensional as they were modelled to surmount the helm. In later heraldry, long after armour had gone out of use, this essential attribute was often forgotten and the result was the granting of 'impractical' crests, that is to say disembodied objects which could in no wise be fitted upon a helm. One such was granted to Sir Francis Drake in 1581 and consists of a ship in full sail being drawn round a terrestrial globe by a hand appearing out of a cloud.

Supporters, the human or animal figures which in a full achievement

N. Bacon eques auratus & magni
sigilli Angliae Custos librum hunc bi-
bliothecae Cantabrig. dicauit.
1574.

The earliest armorial bookplate known in England (earlier examples are to be found on the Continent) is that of Sir Nicholas Bacon (1509–1579), Lord Keeper of the Great Seal under Queen Elizabeth I. It shows the arms of Bacon (gules, on a chief argent two mullets pierced sable) quartering those of Quaplode (barry of six argent and azure, over all a bend gules), with a crescent for difference. The crest is that of Bacon, a boar passant ermine, a rather obvious play on the name. The crest of Quaplode is also a boar passant, blazoned proper. Dated 1574, the bookplate, a hand-coloured woodcut, was probably printed by Richard Tottel of Fleet Street, London, to mark Bacon's gift of some seventy volumes to Cambridge University Library. Sir Nicholas's eldest son, also Nicholas, was the first man to be created a baronet, in 1611, while his son by his second marriage was the celebrated Sir Francis Bacon, later Earl of Verulam, believed by many to be the true author of Shakespeare's plays.

William Faithorne the elder (1616–1691), who was banished from England for refusing to take the oath to Oliver Cromwell, engraved this fine armorial bookplate for Thomas Gore (1632–1684), of Alderton, Wiltshire, a writer on heraldry and sometime friend of John Aubrey. It displays six quarterings: Gore, Whitoxmead, Kennell, Hall, unidentified and White.

This early Scottish armorial bookplate was engraved by Robert Wood, of Edinburgh (fl1700–1722) for Sir James Primrose of Carrington, Baronet, who was created Viscount Primrose on 30 November 1703 and died in 1706. The arms are blazoned as or, on a fesse purpure three primroses of the field, over all a lion rampant vert, armed and langued gules. The crest is a demi-lion gules holding in the dexter paw a primrose proper.

The armorial bookplate of Francis Columbine (c1680–1746), by an unknown engraver, must be dated in or after 1739, the year in which he was promoted to the rank of Lieutenant-General. A fine example of the rococo style, it shows six quarterings with the arms of Master (azure, a fess embattled between three griffins' heads erased or) in pretence.

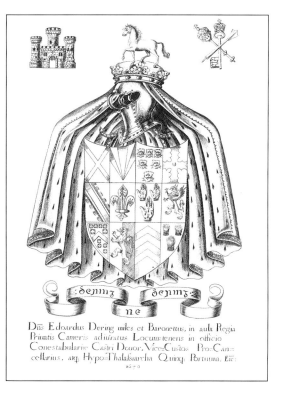

This large armorial bookplate of Thomas Osborne, 1st Duke of Leeds (1632–1712), was engraved in the workshop of William Jackson of London (fl1696–1714). It shows eight quarterings: Osborne, Broughton, Secroft, Hewit, Hewit, Walmesley, Danvers and Nevill.

This armorial bookplate used by Sir Edward Dering, Baronet (1598–1644), antiquary and politican, displays twelve quarterings: Dering, Heyton, Shillingshale, Haut, Surrenden, Pluckley, Malmaynes, Brent, Berkeley, Marshall, Strongbow and Macmurrough.

of arms support the shield on either side, are the prerogative of sovereigns and princes of the blood royal, of peers, of Knights of the Garter and the Thistle, and of Knights Grand Cross of the other orders of knighthood. In a few exceptional cases they have also been granted to baronets and other individuals. Supporters are not found until about the middle of the fourteenth century and undoubtedly derive from the quaint depictions on seals of an earlier period in which shields are often shown suspended from the necks of human figures, animals or birds, and sometimes from the branches of trees.

Badges have never formed an integral part of a coat of arms, but are personal symbols assumed and now occasionally granted as an adjunct to arms. The best-known example is the so-called 'Prince of Wales's Feathers', which Edward, Prince of Wales (the Black Prince), allegedly adopted and adapted (together with the motto *'Ich Dien'* – 'I serve') from

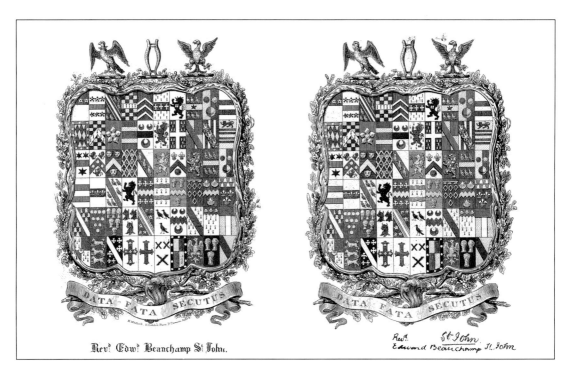

Rev? Edw? Beauchamp S? John.

Rev?
Edward Beauchamp S? John
St John

The elaborate armorial bookplate of the Reverend Edward Beauchamp St John (1795–1856), Rector of Ideford, Devon, from 1844 until his death, shows no less than sixty quarterings. It was engraved by N Whittock of 11 London Place, St Clements, Oxford.

the bearings of the blind King John of Bohemia, defeated and slain at the Battle of Crécy in 1346. An earlier and almost equally well-known example is the sprig of broom which is to be found on the great seal of King Richard I, who took it from the sprig of broom which his grandfather Geoffrey, Count of Anjou (whom we have already encountered in Chapter 1), invariably wore in his cap. The broom plant (*planta genista*) gave rise to Geoffrey's nickname of Plantagenet, which is now generally used as the designation of the dynasty descended from him which ruled England from 1154 to 1485. Contrary to popular belief, however, Plantagenet was not actually used as a surname by any of his descendants until well into the fifteenth century.

Mottoes, now associated in the mind with Christmas crackers, can be in any language and were originally derived from the war-cries or rallying-calls of medieval warriors to their followers. Later they often enshrined a favourite maxim, an expression of piety, or a whimsical play on the family name akin to the canting arms which have already been mentioned.

For definitions and descriptions of the many charges, ordinaries, sub-ordinaries and divisions used in blazonry, the reader is again referred to the Glossary.

The very crudely drawn and engraved book-plate of Selina Hastings, Countess of Huntingdon (1707–1791), is an example of the nadir reached by heraldic art in the eighteenth century. It probably also reflects the Countess's unworldliness and lack of interest in material things. She is remembered as the founder of the Countess of Huntingdon's Connection, an extreme Protestant sect, and her enthusiasm in seeking converts among the nobility led a duchess to write to her: 'It is monstrous to be told that you have a heart as sinful as the common wretches that crawl on the earth. This is highly offensive and insulting, and I cannot but wonder that your Ladyship should relish any sentiments so much at variance with high rank and good breeding.'

The seventeenth-century armorial bookplate of Randolph Egerton, of Betley, Staffordshire, shows the arms of Egerton (sable, a fess ermine between three pheons argent) with a quartered shield in pretence, in which the first and fourth quarters are those of Banning of London 1588 (argent, two bars sable, each charged with as many escallops or), and the second and third have not been identified.

CHAPTER 3

Heralds and the College of Arms

Heralds may be said to predate heraldry by very many centuries, for their original function, as messengers, stems from the high office of *keryx* (Greek) or *caduceator* (Latin), whose duties were to summon persons from far and wide to attend public assemblies, proclaim war and peace, treat with the enemy, and act as confidential servants to kings and rulers. These heralds carried as a symbol of their office staves of olive or laurel wood bound with a carved representation of two entwined snakes (the *caduceus*), which ensured the inviolability of their persons as they went about their duties. When on missions of peace, the snakes were replaced or covered by wool. Under the Roman Empire the office of herald became gradually less exalted and its holders were little more than glorified towncriers (*praecones*).

With the rise of heraldry in twelfth-century Europe, it became necessary to appoint officers to regulate its use and generally oversee the marshalling of arms and the arrangement of jousts and tournaments. Such duties seemed naturally to fall upon the messengers who plied to and fro between the households of kings and great nobles.

In England, although the College of Arms was not incorporated until 1484, kings, heralds and pursuivants of arms in the service of the Crown and of great nobles of the day had been in existence at least since the reign of King Edward I (1272–1307).

For heraldic purposes England was divided into two administrative districts, north and south of the river Trent, by 1276, when a certain Peter (de Herberi ?) is mentioned as *'rex hyraudorum citra acquam de Trente ex parta boriali'*. He is regarded as the first Norroy King of Arms. Later in the reign a Guyenne King of Arms is heard of, with heraldic jurisdiction over England's French possessions. It can be assumed that a king of arms with jurisdiction south of the Trent existed from the same time as Norroy King first appeared to the north and it has been surmised, not unreasonably, that he bore the title of Surroy, but the first person recorded as having such jurisdiction bore the designation of Clarenceux King of Arms and is first mentioned in 1334. The founding of the Order of the Garter in 1348 probably created a need for more heraldic officers to be appointed and

The College of Arms today at Queen Victoria Street, London EC4. The handsome late-seventeenth-century, red-brick building, with the dome of St Paul's Cathedral rising behind it, was rebuilt after the Great Fire of London (1666).

Lancaster and Windsor Heralds are heard of within a few years of the foundation.

Throughout the ensuing century, kings of arms, heralds and pursuivants proliferated, their offices being necessitated by the French Wars and the extremely busy military activities of the warlike Lancastrian and Yorkist monarchs. Weird and wonderful are the designations of some of these officers – Antelope Pursuivant, Blanch Lyon Pursuivant, Comfort Pursuivant, Fleur de lis Herald, Nazers Herald (from Edward III's victory at Najara in 1367), Risebank Pursuivant, Rose Blanche and Rose Rouge Pursuivants, and Vaillant or Volant King of Arms.

The office of Garter King of Arms was established by King Henry V in 1415, the year of Agincourt, and William Bruges (*d*1450) was the first to hold it. From its inception the incumbent was designated not only the King of Arms of the Order of the Garter but also Principal King of Arms for all England, in spite of the fact that Clarenceux and Norroy Kings both antedated him.

It was during the tenure of office of the third Garter, John Writhe, that King Richard III, who as Constable of England during the reign of his brother King Edward IV had gained some knowledge of the heralds' work, granted a charter of incorporation to the officers of arms and gave them a house in the City of London called Coldharbour, situated in what is now Upper Thames Street.

The first College of Arms was shortlived, since after Richard's defeat and death at Bosworth in 1485 the new King Henry VII annulled all his predecessor's acts and the heralds were forced to disperse. They remained without a corporate home until 1555, when Queen Mary I granted them a new charter and a new home, Derby House, on the site of which the present College stands.

In the meantime King Edward VI had established that the College should consist of the Earl Marshal and thirteen officers in ordinary – three kings (Garter, Clarenceux and Norroy), six heralds (Chester, Lancaster, Richmond, Somerset, Windsor and York), and four pursuivants (Bluemantle, Portcullis, Rouge Croix and Rouge Dragon). These thirteen officers have continued to form the College of Arms ever since, augmented from time to time by such extraordinary officers as may be appointed at times of coronations or other important royal events or to enable retired members of the College to retain a footing within its walls.

At the time of writing there are seven extraordinary officers, all heralds (Norfolk, Wales, New Zealand, Surrey, Beaumont, Arundel and Maltravers). The members of the College form part of the royal household and are appointed by Letters Patent under the Great Seal on the recommendation of the Duke of Norfolk as Earl Marshal. They still receive the (now derisory) nominal salaries first fixed in the sixteenth century, but are able to augment these from the private practice of genealogy, which can be lucrative. The heralds and pursuivants take it in turn to be 'in waiting' for a week at a time, during which they deal with all enquiries and any applicant for a grant of arms becomes their personal client so that they receive the fees for the research involved and the design for the arms eventually granted. Each officer is allotted a suite of rooms in the College and some of these are extremely handsome.

It is paradoxical that the final establishment of the College of Arms coincided with the beginning of a long period of decadence and decline in the practice of armory, much deplored by Oswald Barron, from whom we again quote:

> With the false genealogy came in the assumption or assigning of shields to which the new bearers had often no better claim than lay in a surname resembling that of the original owner.

An example of this is to be found in the arms of Earl Spencer (brother of HRH The Princess of Wales), whose ancestor, of perfectly respectable yeoman stock, was granted arms based upon those of the old family of Le Despenser and supplied with a completely fictitious pedigree of descent from them.

Barron also rails against the decadence in heraldic art, citing the 'absurd rule current for some three hundred years', whereby the helmets of princes, baronets and knights are depicted full face and those of peers and gentlemen in profile. This has resulted in the crests of princes and knights ludicrously appearing sideways on a facing helmet. Throughout the eighteenth and well into the nineteenth century, heraldic art was at its lowest ebb. Ugly-shaped shields bore meanly drawn charges, and supporters, instead of resting securely on grassy mounds as heretofore, were perched precariously on weird bracket-like arrangements resembling nothing so much as the wrought-iron contrivances from which flower baskets are often suspended. (The older heraldic writers of Barron's day used to liken them to gas-brackets, but who today has seen a gas-bracket?)

During the sixteenth and seventeenth centuries the lives of the heralds and their families who resided in the College with them were often very far from edifying. They squabbled fiercely among themselves and accounts exist of heralds' wives discharging the contents of their chamberpots on the heads of those who had incurred their displeasure and were unfortunate enough to pass beneath their windows.

In 1595 on Queen Elizabeth I's orders the Commissioners for the Office of Earl Marshal began an enquiry into the sorry state of the College and as a result certain reforms were effected from 1597 onwards. William Camden (1551–1623), the greatest antiquary and historian of the day, was appointed Clarenceux King of Arms and set about the reordering of the library, recovering many volumes which had been purloined by other members of the College. A former usher and later headmaster of Westminster School, Camden had used the school holidays to travel throughout the country collecting antiquarian and archaeological information which was later enshrined in his famous *Britannia*, first published in 1586 and destined to go through six editions in his lifetime. He was also the author of numerous other works, including a transcription of the epitaphs in Westminster Abbey (1600) and a collection of old English chronicles (1603).

A catalogue of the College library was made in 1618, when the books and manuscripts were arranged in twelve presses. The compiler was probably Samson Lennard, Rouge Rose Pursuivant Extraordinary in 1613 and Bluemantle Pursuivant from 1616 until his death in 1633.

The heralds' duties as ambassadors ceased in Elizabeth I's reign (1556–1603) and that of James I (1603–1625) saw the last of jousting, so that the heralds' ceremonial duties were reduced to attendances at coronations, royal funerals, installations and heraldic funerals of the nobility and gentry. The rise of a new and prosperous gentry from Henry VIII's reign (1509–1547) onwards had created a demand for pedigree-making and henceforth the genealogical aspect of the heralds' craft came to the fore. It was an uncritical age as well as being one of credulity and the heralds' clients were given the pedigrees they wanted, supported by faked evidence if necessary, the alleged descent of the Spencers from the Le Despensers being an example already cited. There were, however, a few enlightened spirits (Camden was one) who applied a critical faculty to their work and were not prepared to accept the old wives' tales offered to them as serious family tradition.

A very important aspect of the heralds' work at this time was the Visitations of the counties of England made to record the arms and pedigrees of the nobility and gentry, in the course of which an invaluable corpus of information was gathered in and recorded for posterity.

The Civil War and the subsequent establishment of the Commonwealth caused a disruption in the life of the College. Most of its members remained loyal to the King and accompanied the court to Oxford. Parliament retaliated by declaring the Court of Chivalry (see below) illegal and appointing Edward Bysshe, Member of Parliament for Bletchingley, as Garter in place of Sir Edward Walker. Bysshe was a conscientious and scholarly man, who discharged his duties well, editing several heraldic treatises; but at the Restoration in 1660 Walker was reinstated as Garter, although Bysshe was reappointed as Clarenceux the following year and also knighted. He retained the office until his death in 1679, two years after that of Walker. All the grants of arms made under the Commonwealth were declared void at the Restoration.

The Great Fire of London destroyed the College building in September 1666, but fortunately the heralds had enough warning to enable them to remove all 'except one or two' of their books and manuscripts. A temporary College was set up in part of the Palace of Westminster and remained there until 1674 when they were able to move back to the rebuilt Derby House.

The outstanding figure in the post-Restoration College is undoubtedly Sir William Dugdale (1605–1686), who was appointed Blanch Lyon Pursuivant Extraordinary in 1638, Rouge Croix in 1640, Chester Herald in 1644, Norroy in 1660 and finally Garter in 1677. His literary output approached that of Camden. *Monasticon Anglicanum* was published in 1655; *Antiquities of Warwickshire* in 1656; *History of Imbanking and Drayning of Divers Fenns and Marshes* in 1662; *Origines Juridiciales* in 1666; and his great *Baronage of England*, the forerunner of *Debrett's Peerage*, in 1675–6. Dugdale set out to augment and consolidate the library, collecting together many manuscript volumes himself and persuading other members of the College to donate or bequeath their collections.

From the end of the seventeenth century the College entered a period of decline, Visitations and the fashion for heraldic funerals both coming to an end. Although there were one or two outstanding heralds, notably

SR. WM. DUGDALE.

From an Original in the Bodleian Gallery, Oxford.

Pub. May 1, 1802. by S. Harding, 127, Pall Mall

Sir William Dugdale (1605–1686), the distinguished Garter King of Arms and prolific writer on antiquarian subjects.

John Anstis, Garter from 1715 until his death in 1744, matters did not begin to improve until early in the reign of George III (1760–1820), when the College's activities were boosted by the rise of a prosperous middle class combined with the care taken by Stephen Martin Leake (1703–1773), Garter from 1754, in the selection of suitable candidates for office in the College. Another prominent Garter was Sir Isaac Heard (1730–1822), who held the office from 1784, and whose long reign encompassed the period of the Napoleonic Wars with its profusion of honours bestowed on military and naval commanders, creating much business for the heralds of the day.

The nineteenth and twentieth centuries have witnessed not only the acquisition of a wealth of new material by the College but also a vast improvement in the quality of heraldic art. This last has been brought about very largely by the interest and inspiration of such great figures as Oswald Barron (1868–1939), appointed Maltravers Herald Extraordinary only a year before his death, whom we have already quoted, and Arthur Charles Fox-Davies (1871–1928), who, although never a member of the College, edited both *Dod's Peerage* and *Burke's Landed Gentry* and produced the superbly illustrated *Armorial Families*, running into several editions, *The Art of Heraldry, Heraldry Explained, The Complete Guide to Heraldry*, and several other books of similar nature, as well as works of fiction bearing such titles as *The Dangerous Inheritance, The Mauleverer Murders, The Sex Triumphant*, and *The Troubles of Colonel Marwood*.

In recent years the Heraldry Society, founded in 1947 by Mr John Philip Brooke Brooke-Little, still its distinguished chairman as well as Norroy and Ulster King of Arms since 1980, and its attractively produced quarterly magazine *The Coat of Arms*, have done much for the growing interest in heraldry and genealogy, which now rival stamp- and coin-collecting in popularity as a hobby.

Before passing on to other matters, some mention must be made of the Court of Chivalry, also referred to as the Earl Marshal's Court, a court first set up in the fourteenth century to hear heraldic cases.

The most famous case to come before it was the Scrope versus Grosvenor dispute heard in 1389. Sir Robert le Grosvenor, a rich Cheshire landowner, bore the arms azure, a bend or, and was challenged by Sir Richard le Scrope, lst Lord Scrope of Bolton, who claimed that he and his family alone had the right to bear these arms. The Court was presided over by the Duke of Gloucester as Constable of England and found in favour of Scrope, ordering Grosvenor to difference his arms with a bordure argent. Not content with this judgement, Sir Robert appealed to King Richard II, who not only confirmed Scrope's right to the arms but also disallowed the difference granted to Grosvenor in the original judgement. Sir Robert then assumed the arms azure, a garb or, which have

William Bruges, the first Garter King of Arms, kneeling before St George. Bruges wears his tabard and a very elaborate crown. This interesting illustration is taken from one of the Stowe manuscripts in the British Library.

The arms of the College of Arms surrounded by those of the four Kings of Arms,
Garter, Clarenceux, Norroy and Ulster; from Lant's Roll c1595.

The funeral standard and trophies of Sir John Spencer (d1599). Sir John Spencer was a direct ancestor of the Duke of Marlborough, Earl Spencer and HRH the Princess of Wales. His funeral took place at a time when the heralds held the monopoly for conducting funerals of the nobility and gentry.

A herald's tabard: one of the tabards worn on state occasions by the members of the College of Arms.

been borne by his descendants ever since. As a wry footnote, it may be added that Sir Robert's descendant the 2nd Duke of Westminster (1879–1953) cynically named one of his race horses Bend Or. It became a winner and the Duke himself came to bear the same nickname. In the course of the original controversy a witness deposed that the same arms had also been borne by the ancient but somewhat obscure family of Carminow in Cornwall and their right to do so was not disallowed, or at least not challenged.

The Court of Chivalry continued to hear cases concerning peerage matters and the bearing of arms for some 350 years. Early in the eighteenth century the hall of the College was fitted up as a courtroom and remains almost unaltered to this day, although no cases have been heard there since 1733. After a lapse of 222 years, the Court of Chivalry sat again in 1955, when an action was brought by the Corporation of the City of Manchester against the Manchester Palace of Varieties, complaining that the Corporation arms were unlawfully displayed on a pelmet above the main curtain in their auditorium. The Court sat on 21 December 1955 at the Royal Courts of Justice, the courtroom at the College being deemed too small to accommodate the number of officials, reporters and spectators expected. The Duke of Norfolk, Earl Marshal, presided, with the Lord Chief Justice, Lord Goddard, as his surrogate, and attended by the members of the College in their uniforms. After an amiably conducted hearing, judgement was given in favour of the plaintiff with costs of £300. It was understood that the parties had agreed beforehand to abide by the Court's decision, otherwise it might have been extremely difficult to enforce the judgement. The Court of Chivalry has not sat since, but the review of the laws of arms on which the arguments of Counsel in the case were based has done much to make them better understood and less frequently abused in subsequent years.

CHAPTER 4

Scottish Heraldry
and the Lyon Court

Scottish heraldry differs from English heraldry in very many ways and is not subject to the College of Arms, possessing its own jurisdiction in the Court of the Lord Lyon, which antedates the incorporation of the College by more than a century and a half. It is recorded that in 1318 King Robert I (Robert the Bruce) created a Lyon King of Arms, who was knighted and received a gilt cup and a salary of £100 per annum. (These were 'pounds Scots', worth considerably less than pounds sterling.)

The name of this first Lyon (if indeed he was the first) is not known, nor are those of his immediate successors, but a Lord Lyon is known to have died in 1388, and eleven years later one Henry Grieve is heard of as 'King of Scottish Heralds', although it is not stated whether he was known as Lyon, Rothesay, or Albany. Douglas, 'Herald of the King', occurs from c1410–37, and may have been Lord Lyon, but the unbroken succession commences with Duncan Dundas of Newliston in 1452. His two immediate successors are somewhat shadowy figures, but the third, Sir Andrew Murray of Truim, is a man of more substance and was formerly Albany or Islay Herald.

From this time onwards a great deal is known about the individual Lyons, some of whom were quite colourful figures. One of these was Sir Robert Forman of Luthrie (1555–67), who was deposed for alleged inefficiency, but really for being an adherent of Queen Mary. His successor was Sir William Stewart of Luthrie (1567–8), deposed in his turn for witchcraft and burnt at the stake on 16 August 1569, probably because he was a potential witness in the Kirk o' Field murder of Darnley. His successor, Sir David Lindsay of Rathillet (1568–91), fared better, finally retiring on account of the infirmities of old age in favour of his nephew, Sir David Lindsay of The Mount II (1591–1620). An earlier Sir David Lindsay of The Mount (Lyon 1542–55) not only compiled a Roll of Scottish Arms which is one of the earliest still extant, but was also a notable poet and satirical writer.

Armorial bearings of the late Sir Iain Moncreiffe of that Ilk, 11th Baronet, CVO QC, 24th Chief of the Name and Arms of Moncreiffe. The arms are blazoned as follows. Arms – argent, a lion rampant gules, armed and langued azure, a chief ermine. Crest – on a cap of maintenance gules furred ermine of a Scottish feudal baron, a helmet with mantling vert slashed in an outline of oakleaves and veined or, and out of a crest coronet or (as 24th Chief of the Moncreiffes), a demi-lion rampant as in the arms. Badge – a chaplet of oakleaves proper, fructed of six acorns or, and within it a shoot of mistletoe fructed proper. Supporters – two bearded men proper in armour cap-a-pie sable and having Celtic conical helmets sable banded or, spurs or, swords at their sides hilted or, and in their exterior hands lances paleways gules, the spearheads argent. The badge of a baronet of Nova Scotia is suspended below the shield.

Sir James Balfour of Denmilne and Kinnaird, who has been described as 'probably one of the most accomplished men to hold the office', was appointed Lord Lyon on 17 March 1630, knighted on 2 May, 'crowned' on 15 June 1630, and finally created a Baronet on 22 December 1633. He officiated at the Scottish coronations of Charles I and Charles II, at the latter of which his recital in full of the royal pedigree took one and a half hours to deliver. It was by these recitals that Lyon fulfilled the office of High Sennachie which dated back to the old Celtic Kingdom. Sir James was deprived of his office by Cromwell in 1654 and died on 17 February 1657.

Although many records of the Lyon Court were lost as a result of the Civil War and its aftermath, a succession of vigorous Lyons ensured its continuance as a well-run and efficient body until the appointment of Robert Auriol, 10th Earl of Kinnoull, as Lord Lyon in 1796. He and his son and successor, Thomas Robert, 11th Earl, held office between them for a period of seventy years until the death of the latter in 1866. Neither man had any feeling for heraldry and regarded the office as a sinecure in

The Royal Proclamation of the Queen's coronation being made from the Mercat Cross in Edinburgh. Lyon King of Arms and the officers of his court are grouped on the Cross, which is situated behind St Giles's Cathedral on the Royal Mile. The Proclamation is being read by the aged Sir Francis Grant, Albany Herald, anxiously watched by Sir Thomas Innes of Learney, who had succeeded him as Lord Lyon in 1945.

which he might sell heraldships and pursuivancies to the highest bidders, usually men who cared for or knew as little of heraldry as himself.

This sorry state of affairs led to the setting up of a Commission of Enquiry under Lord Cornwallis following the death of the 11th Earl in February 1866. Up until this time there were six heralds (Albany, Rothesay, Marchmont, Snowdoun, Ross and Islay) and six pursuivants (Carrick, Unicorn, Dingwall, Bute, Ormonde and Kintyre) subordinate to the Lord Lyon. As a result of the Commission's findings the Lyon Court Act was passed in 1867 and the subordinate officers were reduced to three of each rank.

At the time of writing the three existing heralds are entitled Albany, Rothesay and Ross, and there are two pursuivants, Kintyre and Unicorn, with one vacancy. Heraldic humorists like to tell of an overheard telephone conversation between a pursuivant and his superior which opened as follows: 'Hello, is that you Lyon? This is Unicorn speaking.'

This century has seen three great Lyons: Sir James Balfour Paul KCVO (1890–1926), the author of many heraldic treatises as well as being editor of the monumental nine-volume work *The Scots Peerage*; Sir Francis James Grant KCVO (1929–45), also an author, whose *The Manual of Heraldry* ran into several editions, and who held heraldic office from his appointment as Carrick Pursuivant in 1886 until his death as Albany Herald in 1953 (having resigned as Lyon in 1945), a period only two months short of sixty-seven years; and Sir Thomas Innes of Learney GCVO (1945–69), the author of two great textbooks, *Scots Heraldry* and *The Clans, Septs and Regiments of the Scottish Highlands*. Sir Thomas delighted in affecting a broad Scots accent on occasion and once admonished a young visitor, who, at breakfast, spread his marmalade straight on to his toast instead of depositing it politely at the side of his plate, with the words: 'There's no' a war on the nu!' The present Lord Lyon (since 1981) is Sir Thomas Innes of Learney's son, Sir Malcolm Rognvald Innes of Edingight KCVO.

No account of the Scottish heraldic establishment would be complete without some mention being made of that very much loved figure Sir Iain Moncreiffe of that Ilk, 11th Baronet, CVO, Kintyre Pursuivant (1953–61) and later Albany Herald (1961–85), whose untimely death deprived the world of a wit and scholar of quite extraordinary proportions. Every one of his writings is a polished and elegant masterpiece of erudition, spiced with the most amusing digressions. Some of the best of these have been gathered together in a memorial volume, *Lord of the Dance*, edited by Hugh Montgomery-Massingberd.

In Scotland it is the Lord Lyon who makes grants of arms, that prerogative having been committed to him from the Crown by the Court of Session since 1542. He is a judge in all matters relating to genealogies, the chiefship of clans, chieftaincies within clans, and headship of families, often very controversial matters.

Unlike England, the grant of a coat of arms in Scotland confers nobility, and grantees are referred to in the wording of their grants as being 'received as nobles in the noblesse of Scotland'. Again unlike England, Scottish arms are not heritable by all the male line descendants of the original grantee, but pass down by order of primogeniture, the cadets being obliged to matriculate their own arms, suitably differenced from the paternal coat. As in England, the salaries of the Scottish heraldic officers are nominal, having been fixed in 1694 at £25 per annum for heralds and £16 for pursuivants, and are made up by fees from clients.

The main duties of the Lyon Court today are the granting of arms both public and private, the recording of pedigrees and their entry in *The Public Register of All Genealogies and Birth Briefs in Scotland*, and the organization of state ceremonies such as the opening of the General Assembly of the Church of Scotland, proclamations of royal accessions and so on from the Mercat Cross in Edinburgh, Order of the Thistle services and installations, and installations of governors of Edinburgh Castle.

CHAPTER 5

Modern Heraldry
and its Usage Today

Heraldry is as relevant to modern life as it was in the Middle Ages and although it has seen several periods of decadence it remains an unchanging science which has been perfected and purified over the years into the pleasing art form it presents today. The steady decline which began in the reign of Queen Elizabeth I and reached its height in the middle of the eighteenth century with the vogue for pictorial designs completely alien to the more abstract styles of medieval heraldry, was only arrested by the Gothic revival in the nineteenth century and the pre-Raphaelite influence on art towards the end of Queen Victoria's reign. Barron and Fox-Davies, although not always seeing eye-to-eye, were the two persons most instrumental in bringing about the healthy reformation in heraldic art and practice. The former, whom we have already quoted more than once, was the champion of a return to the purer and simpler forms of the Middle Ages, while the latter advocated a revitalized and new style of design which has influenced all heraldic artists to this day.

Arthur George Maynard Hesilrige, who was editor of *Debrett's Peerage and Baronetage* from 1887 to 1935 and remained consulting editor until his death in 1953 in his ninetieth year, had much sound advice to offer to the aspiring heraldic artist in *Debrett's Heraldry*, which appeared under his editorship in 1914. His first chapter, entitled 'Hints on Heraldic Depiction', although slightly dated, is well worth reproducing in part here:

> Generally speaking, nine points must be borne in mind:-
>
> (1) – Always read the blazon through before commencing work. It is a common thing to find when one has mapped out a coat that there is a Chief to be included, or that a Supporter is 'collared and chained and charged on the shoulder'. Bear in mind that a Baronet (unless his title be of Nova Scotia creation) has the Ulster badge charged on the shield, and when planning the design, leave a space for it. These charges never look nice if they have to be painted in over other work, and no matter how correct the practice is in theory,

in actual fact the ensuing result is bad.

(2) – Always complete the whole design in pencil. Mantling which looks well on one side may be impossible to balance on the other, particularly should one supporter be a horned beast, and the other not. In such a case, should half the mantling have been completed, the artist will find himself in an awkward predicament.

(3) – Don't despise mechanical aid. Use compasses, T-square, and set-square whenever possible. It may take longer, but the result will be better. A Viscount's coronet drawn freehand cannot be compared with one drawn with a bow pen.

(4) – Lay all your colours in flat tints. A little Chinese white mixed with the colour greatly facilitates matters. Always use the same colour throughout. If a field is gules, don't use vermilion for the shield and crimson for the mantling. Ink in your outlines after the tinctures and shadings have been worked in. For actual outlining a thin, flat-pointed brush is preferable to a pen – it does not scratch up the colour. Always use Waterproof Indian Ink. Avoid erasures, but if ink work has to be rubbed out, a good typewriter rubber is better than a knife – it does not cut so deeply into the surface.

(5) – Don't attempt too much. The simpler the design, the more pleasing is the finished work to the eye. Too much shading will throw the charges into high relief, and that is not desirable. An actual shield has the design painted on in flat colours, and is not ornamented in bas-relief. Generally speaking, the light should strike the shield from the top left. The high lights should come on the dexter side, and the heavier shadows on the sinister.

(6) – If gold leaf or kindred substances which require burnishing are used, lay them on first. This will avoid the danger of the rubbing with the agate burnisher damaging the colour work.

(7) – Be very careful with the lettering of the motto. If Old English lettering is used, see that it is Old English and not a bastard mixture of Gothic and Norman.

(8) – Don't make the charges too small. Let them more or less fill the available space.

(9) – Above all, never hurry. A good drawing wants to be executed with all the care and trouble that the old illuminators used to exercise. One slip, and hours of work can easily be neutralised.

In conclusion, bear in mind that clearness and distinctness are essential in emblazoning a coat of arms.

Those who follow Mr Hesilrige's precepts stand a good chance of becoming fairly competent heraldic artists after a little practice.

As has already been said, modern heraldic grants have been of a consistently high standard and those which have been made to corporate bodies such as banks and building societies are often boldly displayed on the walls of head offices and branches alike and provide spirited and colourful contributions to enliven every high street.

A good example of modern heraldic design, incorporating several traditional features which have already been mentioned, is provided by the arms granted on 16 April 1988 to Mr Derek Albert Tooke, who has very kindly agreed that they may be used as an illustration. The arms are blazoned thus: 'Per chevron Argent and Gules three Griffins' Heads erased counterchanged langued Azure on a Chief also Gules a Pair of Keys saltirewise Or between two Bezants.' The crest is: 'A Mount Vert thereon a Griffin segreant Or armed and langued Gules holding in the dexter claw a Quill Pen and in the sinister claw a Pair of Scales also Gules.'

The choice of shield was based on two factors. The earliest arms on record for Toke (an earlier form of the name) are those recorded for an Essex knight in a roll of arms dating from the time of King Henry VI and published in Joseph Foster's *Some Feudal Coats of Arms* (1902). These were 'per chevron sable and argent, three gryphons' heads erased and counterchanged'. Mr Tooke felt these arms to be very appropriate because the griffin is also the badge of the Midland Bank (the sign of 'The Guinea and Griffin'), by whom he was employed for some forty years. The shield was differenced by altering the tinctures to argent and gules instead of sable and argent. The chief gules is taken from the arms of Norfolk County Council. All Mr Tooke's paternal ancestors, as far as can be traced, came from that county, as well as some of his maternal ancestors. It is also the colour on the shield of the Chartered Institute of Bankers (of which Mr Tooke is a Fellow), plus the two bezants, which, of course, represent coins. The crossed keys were suggested by Mr Patric Dickinson, Richmond Herald, as a play on the name Tooke, and to Mr Tooke these also symbolize the keys which he carried on the Midland Bank's behalf for most of his business career ('Very inconvenient too, on many occasions,' is his added comment).

The crest, a griffin, set on a green mount to represent Mr Tooke's rural background, carries a quill pen to indicate an administrative occupation and a pair of scales, indicating not only that Mr Tooke is a Justice of the Peace, but also harking back to his early days in banking when a set of scales was an invaluable tool for a cashier.

For his motto Mr Tooke chose 'Freedom With Duty', which he says is, as he feels, the freedom to do some of the things which were difficult for him to do when he was in full-time employment, but which he may now do within the constraints imposed upon him by family and society.

This very pleasing achievement of Derek Tooke displays the best elements of the timeless science of heraldry applied to the life and career of a modern businessman.

ALL AND SINGULAR *to whom these Presents shall come, Sir Alexander Colin Cole, Knight Commander of the Royal Victorian Order, upon whom has been conferred the Territorial Decoration, Garter Principal King of Arms and Sir Anthony Richard Wagner, Knight Commander of the Most Honourable Order of the Bath, Knight Commander of the Royal Victorian Order, Clarenceux King of Arms, Send Greeting! WHEREAS DEREK ALBERT TOOKE of Mount Vale Woodside Close, Caterham in the County of Surrey, Esquire, Fellow of the Chartered Institute of Bankers, Freeman of the City of London, in the Commission of the Peace for the County of Surrey, hath represented unto The Most Noble Miles Francis Stapleton, Duke of Norfolk, Knight of the Most Noble Order of the Garter, Knight Grand Cross of the Royal Victorian Order, Companion of the Most Honourable Order of the Bath, Commander of the Most Excellent Order of the British Empire, upon whom has been conferred the Decoration of the Military Cross, Earl Marshal and Hereditary Marshal of England, that he is desirous of having Letters Patent of Armorial Bearings granted and appointed unto him and duly recorded in Her Majesty's College of Arms and hath requested therefore the favour of His Grace's Warrant for Our granting and assigning such Arms and Crest as We deem suitable, to be borne and used by him and his descendants with their due and proper differences and according to the Laws of Arms. And forasmuch as the said Earl Marshal did by Warrant under his hand and Seal bearing date the Twenty-first day of August 1987 authorize and direct Us to grant and assign such Arms and Crest accordingly, Know Ye therefore that We the said Garter and Clarenceux in pursuance of His Grace's Warrant and by virtue of the Letters Patent of Our several Offices granted by The Queen's Most Excellent Majesty to each of Us respectively do by these Presents grant and assign unto the said DEREK ALBERT TOOKE the Arms following that is to say Per chevron Argent and Gules three Griffins Heads erased counterchanged langued Azure on a Chief also Gules a Pair of Keys saltirewise Or between two Bezants And for the Crest upon a Helm with a Wreath Argent and Gules A Mount Vert thereon a Griffin segreant Or armed and langued Gules holding in the dexter claw a Quill Pen and in the sinister claw a Pair of Scales also Gules Mantled Gules doubled Argent as are in the margin hereof more clearly depicted to be borne and used for ever hereafter by the said DEREK ALBERT TOOKE and by his descendants with due and proper differences and according to the Laws of Arms In witness whereof We the said Garter and Clarenceux have to these Presents subscribed Our names and affixed the Seals of Our several Offices this Sixteenth day of April in the Thirty-seventh year of the Reign of Our Sovereign Lady Elizabeth the Second by the Grace of God of the United Kingdom of Great Britain and Northern Ireland and of Her other Realms and Territories Queen, Head of the Commonwealth, Defender of the Faith, and in the Year of Our Lord One Thousand Nine Hundred and Eighty Eight.*

Derek Tooke's grant of arms. This is the usual form of letters patent granting a coat of arms. The arms of the grantee are in the top left-hand corner and the other arms are those (from left to right) of the Duke of Norfolk, Earl Marshal, the Queen, and the College of Arms.

Derek Tooke's coat of arms.

The Arms of His Most Eminent Highness the Prince and Grand Master of the Sovereign Military Hospitaller Order of St John of Jerusalem, of Rhodes and of Malta. Frà Andrew Willoughby Ninian Bertie was elected to this august position in 1988 and as such ranks as a sovereign prince. He is the grandson of the 7th Earl of Abingdon.

CHAPTER 6

Continental Heraldry

Although heraldry originated at roughly the same time all over Europe, its development differed from country to country and this chapter gives a brief resumé, moving from west to east across the Continent.

Spain

Heraldry first appeared in Spain at the beginning of the eleventh century and its origin was the same as in other European countries, namely the need for nobles and knights to distinguish themselves from each other. Originally the coats of arms were rather simple, but during the course of time they became more and more complex, especially the arms granted to the Spanish Conquistadores during the reign of Carlos I (the Holy Roman Emperor Charles V). Until the end of the Middle Ages only the paternal arms were used, but thereafter both paternal and maternal were used, the arms of the paternal and maternal grandfathers being impaled. During the eighteenth and nineteenth centuries the use of four quarterings (1 – paternal grandfather, 2 – maternal grandfather, 3 – paternal grandmother and 4 – maternal grandmother) came into use among the Spanish nobility and by the latter half of the eighteenth century even the use of sixteen quarterings was quite widespread. Examples can be seen today in the northern regions of Spain, the Basque provinces and the former Kingdom of Navarre in stone-carved coats of arms. The ideal proof of *hidalguía* (nobility) is still today the four quarterings.

The office of King of Arms originated in that of the heralds whose job was to determine the arms which each noble family was entitled to use. The functions and duties of the Kings of Arms were clearly defined in the regulations given by King Philip II in 1593, King Carlos III in 1761 and King Carlos IV in 1802, and also by the Royal Decree of King Alfonso XIII in 1915 and by the Decree of 1951, which is still in force. To be a Chronicler-King of Arms (*Cronista-Rey de Armas*) the candidate must hold a degree in law or philosophy and appointments are made by the Minister of Justice, all documents regarding genealogical and heraldic matters being required to be registered and signed by the Under Secretary at the Ministry.

A peculiarity of Spanish heraldry is the use of bordures charged with saltires or shells, and the lack of crests, normally helmets being adorned with plumes only. Mottoes are also rarely found.

The foremost work on Spanish genealogy and heraldry is the monumental work by Arturo and Alberto García Carraffa, *Enciclopedia Heráldica y Genealógica Hispano-Americana*. Also very useful is *Nobiliario Español – Diccionario Heráldico de Apellidos Españoles y de Títulos Nobiliarios* (Madrid, 1954) by Julio de Atienza, Barón de Cobos de Belchite, and perhaps the best-known book on the subject is *Tratado de Heráldica y Blasón* (1929) by José Asensio y Torres. The current Chronicler-King of Arms, Don Vicente de Cadenas y Vicent, a great authority on the Emperor Charles V, has published a considerable amount on genealogical, heraldic and nobiliary matters.

Portugal

Heraldry developed in Portgual at the same time as in Spain, but it was not until the fifteenth century that heralds were first appointed, by King John I (1385–1433). An interesting feature of Portuguese heraldry was the rule that only nobles might use metals (or and argent) in their arms, as many burghers and peasants also used armorial bearings, and it was not until 1512 that King Manuel I absolutely forbade the use of arms to any except the nobility.

A splendid record of Portuguese heraldry was made by the Portugal King of Arms, João du Cros, and entitled *Livro do Armeiro-Mor*. It remains the best work on the heraldry of Portuguese noble families. The records of the Portuguese nobility and their arms are kept in the Arquivo Nacional da Torre do Tombo in Lisbon. Arms and all nobiliary matters were controlled by the heralds until the fall of the monarchy in 1910, but in 1945 the Conselho de Nobreza was formed under the authority of HRH The Duke of Bragança, head of the royal house of Portugal.

Portuguese heraldic rules are similar to those of Scotland as far as the matriculation of arms is concerned, but also made use of the Spanish system of using four quarterings. A very useful work is *Armaria Portuguesa* (1917) by Anselmo Braamcamp Freire, unfortunately unfinished because of the author's death. Other publications are the *Anuario da Nobreza de Portugal*, published by the Istituto Portugues de Heraldica, and *Armorial Lusitano*, published by the Editorial Enciclopedia (Lisbon, 1961), under the direction of Dr Afonso Eduardo Martins Zúquete.

The Associação da Nobreza Histórica de Portugal (at Praça do Principe Real 24, 1200 Lisbon) was founded in 1984 under the high patronage of HRH Dom Duarte, Duke of Bragança, head of the royal house of Portugal (son of the Duke mentioned above).

France

The language of heraldry is French, but sadly, because of the political upheavals of the last two hundred years and the fact that French heraldry is entirely unregulated, the subject is largely unknown to the vast majority of French people. One of the main causes for this unfortunate state of affairs was the failure of the French heralds to fight for a strong position for themselves. Heralds had no power to grant arms and most of their functions were allowed to lapse. In 1615 King Louis XIII created the office of *juge général d'armes de France*. Unfortunately, however, these *juges d'armes* had no power to grant arms, that right being reserved exclusively for the sovereign.

Both nobles and bourgeoisie used arms and it was impossible to tell one from the other. By the end of the thirteenth century the use of heraldry by non-noble persons was fairly widespread.

In 1407 King Charles VI (1380–1422) created a College of Heralds in Paris with three classes of officer: kings of arms, herald and pursuivant, the last being a kind of apprentice. In 1489 King Charles VIII (1483–1498) appointed a herald as *maréchal d'armes des Français* to deal with the arms of the French nobility, and in 1615 King Louis XIII (1610–1643) appointed a *juge général d'armes de France*, who also held the office of *conseilleur du Roi*, and whose position resembled in some ways that of Lord Lyon in Scotland. From 1641 until the Revolution this office remained in the d'Hozier family. In 1696 an edict of King Louis XIV (1643–1715) appointed masters to register arms in their own areas, the main reason behind this being the need for money to meet the ever-rising cost of his interminable campaigns. As may be imagined, the edict was not popular.

In 1790 the use of titles of nobility, arms and liveries was abolished, but they came into use again during the Consulate and in 1802 the *Légion d'Honneur* order was founded. When Napoleon Bonaparte was proclaimed Emperor of the French in 1804 a new nobility was born with the creation of a multitude of princes, dukes, counts, barons and knights, although the members of the old nobility were not allowed to use their titles. The armorial bearings of the newly created nobles usually bore items related to the offices of the holders. After the restoration of the legitimate sovereign Louis XVIII (1814–1824) the old titles were again recognized and the new ones allowed to continue. All titles were again abolished under the Second Republic (1848–1852), although the use of arms was not specifically mentioned. During the Second Empire of Napoleon III (1852–1870) the Statute of 1808 regulating the use of arms under Napoleon I was again in force. The Third, Fourth and Fifth Republics have passed no legislation regarding arms. Civic heraldry is now controlled by the Ministry of the Interior and National Education.

The most up-to-date work on French genealogy and heraldry is the seven-volume *Grand Armorial de France* by Henri Jougla de Morenas. There is quite a number of genealogical and heraldic centres in France, including the Académie Internationale d'Héraldique, the Fédération des Sociétés Françaises de Généalogie, and the Société Française d'Heraldique et de Sigillographie.

Belgium

Heraldry in Belgium developed at the same time as the rest of Europe and is very much in evidence today as this small country possesses a large number of noble families in proportion to its population. Many of these owe their titles to the kings of Spain, who ruled Belgium and the Netherlands as a result of the marriage in 1496 of Archduke Philip of Austria, the heir of the Duchy of Burgundy, to the Spanish Infanta Juana of Aragon, daughter and heiress of Queen Isabel of Castile and King Fernando of Aragon. Other titles were created by the Austrian branch of the House of Habsburg who were also the Holy Roman Emperors. All titles of nobility had to be created or recognized by the sovereign following the edict on heraldic usage of King Philip II of Spain as ruler of the Low Countries in 1598.

The titles in current use are prince, duke, marquis, count, viscount, baron and knight (*chevalier*). Apart from the nobility, burgher and civic arms exist. King Leopold I (1831–1865) established by Royal Decree of 6 February 1844 a Conseil Héraldique, which deals with the verification of titles, heraldry and other nobiliary matters. The Conseil keeps up to date the rolls of nobility, letters patent, and copies of genealogies and arms. An excellent book on Belgian heraldry is *Armorial Général de la Noblesse Belge* (Liège, 1954) by Baron de Ryckman de Betz.

Luxembourg

Heraldry has played an important role in the chequered history of this little country, once part of the Duchy of Burgundy and later ruled by the French, the Spanish and the Austrians. During the Congress of Vienna (1814–15) it was made a Grand Duchy and was held by the Kingdom of the Netherlands until 1890, when it became independent under Duke Adolphe of Nassau.

Most of the genealogical and heraldic records of the Grand Duchy are kept in the Archives Royales, Département de la Noblesse, in Brussels, Belgium.

The Luxembourg Heraldic Society was founded in 1947 and later became Les amies de l'histoire; one of its sections, Le Conseil Héraldique, deals with heraldry, sigillography (seals) and other symbols. An outstanding book on Luxembourg heraldry is *Armorial du Pays de Luxembourg* by Jean-Claude Loutsch.

The Netherlands

The use of heraldry is quite widespread in the Kingdom of the Netherlands by both noble and burgher families and there is no legislation regarding the use of unregistered arms except for those of noble families.

The Hoge Raad van Adel organization in The Hague advises the Queen in all matters regarding nobility, coats of arms, flags of provinces, towns and villages, the badges of the army, navy and air force, and the nobiliary proofs required for admission to the Sovereign Military Order of Malta, the Teutonic Order, and the Johanniter Order in the Netherlands.

There are several genealogical and heraldic societies and also the Centraal Bureau voor Genealogie (at Prins Willem-Alexanderhof 22, 2595 BE 's-Gravenhage), which publishes the *Nederlands Adelsboek* periodically.

Denmark

In Denmark the arms of the untitled noble families tend to be very simple while those of the titled ones are usually complicated by a number of quarterings, helmets and supporters. A special feature is the use of flags or banners as crests. A superb display of arms can be admired in the Chapel of the Orders of the Elephant and the Dannebrog in Frederiksborg Castle, where the arms of the knights are displayed.

The *Danmarks Adels Aarbog* is a regular publication by Poul Kristensen Grafisk Virksomhed, Copenhagen, and gives up-to-date genealogies and arms of the Danish noble families. Also very useful is a charming little book by the late Sven Tito Åchen, *Danske Adelsvabener* (En Heraldik Nogle, Copenhagen, 1973).

Norway

Heraldry has been known in Norway for more than seven hundred years and one of its characteristics is its sheer simplicity, although its usage is rather rare and mainly relegated to the arms of cities and municipalities, there being no titled families.

The best reference works on Norwegian heraldry are the *Lexicon over Adelige Familier i Danmark Norge of Hertugdommerne* (Copenhagen, 1782–1813), and a paper given at the Ninth International Congress of

Genealogy and Heraldry in 1968 by Hans A K T Cappelen in collaboration with Didrik R Heyerdahl, entitled *Norske Slektsvapen* (Norwegian family coats of arms).

Sweden

The House of Nobles (Riddarhuset) in Stockholm is justly regarded as one of the most beautiful buildings in northern Europe. It houses a superb collection of the armorial bearings of the Swedish nobility displayed on the walls of its main council chamber. The House of Nobles is not only a building, but an institution, the nobility as a corporate body. It was first constituted in 1626 and its statute was last renewed in 1866. Meetings of the nobility take place every three years and each noble family has a vote, which is exercised by its head. The *Ridderskapet och Adeln* (chivalry and nobility) continue to exercise a collective interest in the administration of funds for needy members and in maintaining the House of Nobles, where all records and genealogies are kept.

An official, known as the *Riksheraldiker*, is responsible for drawing up and checking new arms. The *Sveriges Ridderskap och Adels Kalender*, which gives an up-to-date genealogy of all members of the Swedish nobility with illustrations of their arms, is published biennially in Stockholm.

Not far from the House of Nobles is the Riddareholmskyrkan, which contains not only a magnificent series of royal tombs, but also the arms of the knights of the Order of the Seraphim painted on metal plates hung around the church.

Finland

Finland was ruled by the kings of Sweden from 1157 to 1809, when it was ceded to Russia and, as a Grand Duchy, became part of the vast Russian Empire, only becoming independent in 1918. After an abortive attempt to make it a kingdom, it became a republic, which it still remains. The Finnish nobility managed to survive all these vicissitudes and the House of Nobles (Finlands Riddarhus), founded in 1816, still flourishes and publishes *Finlands Adels och Ridderskaps Kalender* triennially. There is also a Finnish Society of Genealogists, founded in 1917, which possesses a very large library and publishes a yearbook entitled *Vuosikirja-Arsskrift*.

Germany

No other country in Europe possesses a richer and more colourful heraldic heritage than Germany, with its splended mosaic of electorates, kingdoms, grand duchies, duchies and principalities, to say nothing of the Holy Roman Empire which presided over the whole nation for a thousand years. The very word 'blazon' is possibly of German origin, meaning 'blow the horn'.

Coats of arms may be seen all over Germany, many of them dating from the very early days of heraldry. A characteristic of German heraldry is the use of figures (armed men for example) and a multiplicity of crests, chiefly used to distinguish one branch of a family from another. The arms of noble families are distinguished from those of burghers by a barred

The armorial bookplate (1903) of Philipp Ernst, 7th Prince of Hohenlohe-Schillingsfürst (1853-1915), provides a fine example of German heraldry with its many quarterings and crests. The paternal coat of the Hohenlohes, argent, two leopards passant sable, appears on the dexter side of the shield.

helmet, which became exclusive to the nobility in the 1550s. Heraldic coronets were introduced about one hundred years later.

The best sources for German genealogy and heraldry are the famous *Almanach de Gotha* (published annually from 1763 to 1944) and its successor the *Genealogisches Handbuch des Adels*, published by C A Starke at Limburg a d Lahn, which since 1951 has regularly published separate volumes covering the royal and princely families, counts, barons and untitled nobility. Each volume contains several fine illustrations of family arms.

A twelfth-century German knight in full armour, including helm with peacock crest. His arms are emblazoned on his surcoat, his caparisoned horse and his banner, which he carries in his right hand.

Mention must also be made of the monumental work by J Siebmacher, *Grosses und Allgemeines Wappenbuch* (Nuremberg, 1854), and a very useful periodical, *Der Herold*. A number of regional family history societies also exist throughout Germany.

Austria

In spite of its long history and the prominent part played by its nobility, Austria has never possessed an office or centre for the recording of arms. The public records, however, contain much evidence of arms being granted, both with and without nobility attached. Under the Holy Roman Emperor Francis I (1745–1765), husband of the Habsburg heiress Maria Theresa, a decree was issued forbidding non-nobles to bear arms. Ennoblement and new grants of arms were made until the end of the monarchy in 1919.

The Heraldisch-Genealogische Gessellschaft Adler (at Haarhof 4, Vienna II, Austria), founded in 1870, publishes a useful periodical, *Adler Zeitschrift fur Genealogie und Heraldik*.

A good reference book on Austrian and Hungarian heraldry is *Oesterreichisch-Ungarische Wappenrolle* by Hugo Gerard Ströhl, published at Vienna in 1894 (second edition 1899).

Hungary

Heraldry started in Hungary much later than in the rest of Europe, for it was not until the beginning of the fifteenth century when arms first appeared there. This was after the Hungarian nobles who accompanied their King Sigismund (also Holy Roman Emperor) to the Council of Constance (1414–18) had been impressed by the display of coats of arms which they saw there and decided to adopt their own. However these were never registered anywhere.

It was only in 1526 that arms were matriculated in the *Libri Regii*, and thereafter a central register for arms was kept for Hungary and Transylvania until 1867, when a national archive was established in Budapest.

A very distinctive feature of Hungarian heraldry is the use of Turks' heads, a result of the long struggle against the Muslim invaders who menaced eastern and central Europe for many centuries. The genealogies and arms of many Hungarian families can be found in the publications of C A Starke already mentioned (see 'Germany').

Bohemia

Perhaps the oldest recorded Bohemian coat of arms is that of Vratislav II, who received the title of King for life in 1085 as a personal mark of favour from the Emperor Henry IV. He bore a crowned silver lion on a red field.

Bohemia passed to the Habsburgs in 1526 following the marriage of the heiress, Anna, to the Archduke Ferdinand of Austria, later Emperor Ferdinand I (1556–1564), and thereafter all grants of arms and nobility issued from Vienna and were registered there until 1918. The archives of the National Museum in Prague contain much heraldic material.

Switzerland

The use of heraldry in Switzerland dates from the thirteenth century and there is scarcely a town or small village which does not possess a coat of arms but, in spite of this, there is no official or state herald or heraldic authority. That the Swiss have a great interest in heraldry, nonetheless, is evidenced by the many souvenirs and postcards bearing cantonal and civic coats of arms which are on sale throughout the country. The country is also particularly rich in magnificent heraldic stained glass.

There is a Swiss heraldry society, La Société Suisse d'Héraldique/Schweizer Heraldischen Gesellschaft (at Zwinglistrasse 28, St Gallen), which publishes a well-produced quarterly, *Archives Héraldiques Suisses*.

Italy

With its great artistic past, Italy possesses a wealth of heraldic treasures going back to the very beginning of heraldry. A significant feature of Italian arms is the use by a large number of noble families of the label and three fleurs-de-lis and the crowned eagle in chief to indicate that they supported either the Pope or the Emperor (the opposing parties being known as 'Guelfs' and 'Ghibellines').

The Collegio Araldico (at Istituto Araldico Romano, 00186 Via Santa Maria dell'Anima, 16 Rome, Italy) was founded in 1863 and publishes a periodical, the *Rivista Araldica*, and at intervals the *Libro d'Oro della Nobiltà Italiana*, which is very similar to the *Almanach de Gotha* (see 'Germany').

Two excellent reference works on the heraldry and history of Italian noble families are Marchese Vitorio Spreti's dictionary and Mannucci's five-volume *Nobiliario e Blasonario del Regno d'Italia* (published by the Collegio Araldico in 1928).

The Italian titles of nobility are principe, duca, marchese, conte, visconte, barone, signore and nobile. Since Italy became a republic in 1946 there has been no protection against the usurpation of arms and titles.

Poland

Polish heraldry is quite different from that of the rest of Europe and since it is of runic character it can be assumed that the nobility is of Viking or Scandinavian origin. By the fourteenth century the nobility had become a very well-organized caste. Arms were never personal to the bearers and were used by all the members of a family and frequently by many families with different names and not necessarily with the same origin. It is not known if Polish arms originated as family or clan emblems as in Scotland.

The most distinctive features of Polish heraldry are simplicity and the frequent use of gules and azure. The most common charges are crosses, arrows, crescents and horseshoes. The Polish nobility (szlachta) has its origin in the clan system and differs from the rest of western Europe by being a closed one, since a law passed in 1572 deprived the king of the power to create further nobles. In the fourteenth century Poland and Lithuania were united and the nobility increased in numbers as many Lithuanian families became incorporated into the Polish nobility.

Many Polish nobles received titles from the Holy Roman Emperor, the Russian Emperor, or the Pope. The titles in use are those of prince, marquis, count, baron and knight, and there is a large number of untitled nobility. The best reference work on Polish heraldry is Simon Konarski's *Armorial de la Noblesse Polonaise Titrée*, published at Paris under the patronage of the Académie Internationale d'Héraldique in 1954.

Latvia and Estonia

Latvian heraldry has been very much influenced by that of Germany, chiefly because most of its noble families are of German origin and many descend from the knights of the Teutonic Order. From 1721 until 1918 Latvia and Estonia formed part of the Russian Empire and the Baltic nobility distinguished itself by its loyalty to the Romanoff Dynasty. During the period from 1918 until 1940, when Latvia was occupied by the Communists, a Heraldic Committee was set up under the patronage of the President of the Republic and dealt mainly with municipal arms, although it was assumed that the registration of the arms of noble families would follow eventually.

A German organization, Verband der Angehorigen der Baltischen Ritterschaften, concerns itself with the genealogy and heraldry of Baltic noble families.

The coat of arms of the Russian Counts Bobrinskoy. Alexei Grigorievitch Bobrinskoy (1762–1813) was the illegitimate son of Empress Catherine the Great (1726–1796) and her lover Prince Grigori Grigorievitch Orloff (1734–1783). His surname was derived from the country estate of Bobriki which was given to him by his mother in 1765 and he was created a Count of the Russian Empire by his halfbrother Emperor Paul I just six days after the death of their mother. The coat of arms borne by him and his descendants alludes to his ancestry and combines the arms of Orloff (parted per pale argent and azure, an eagle displayed counterchanged), Bobriki (parted per fess argent and gules, a beaver (in Russian *bobr*) rampant counterchanged), and Anhalt, Catherine the Great's paternal family (argent, on a wall gules a bear passant sable, crowned or), with the Russian imperial eagle on an inescutcheon of pretence and repeated for the crest. The motto translated is 'Glory to God; life to thee', which are said to have been the first words uttered by the Empress after she gave birth to Alexei. There is a story (probably apocryphal) that in order to escape detection by Catherine's husband, Peter III, the baby was smuggled out of the Winter Palace in St Petersburg hidden inside a beaver muff, which certainly provides a more romantic derivation of the surname he later bore.

Lithuania

Heraldry in Lithuania started rather later than in most other European countries and the use of coats of arms did not become widespread until 1413.

The arms of the Grand Duchy of Lithuania, a knight on a white horse, were quartered with the crowned white eagle of Poland after the two countries became united.

Following the third partition of Poland, Lithuania passed under Russian control in 1796 and most of its genealogical and heraldic records were taken to St Petersburg.

There was an attempt to form an association of the Lithuanian nobility in 1928, but it was suppressed by the Soviet rulers. It is not known if this has been revived since *Glasnost*.

Russia

Heraldry was practically unknown in Russia before Peter the Great (1689–1725) and like many other things was born out of his desire to westernize his country. During his travels in Europe he had noticed the widespread use of armorial bearings in churches, stained glass, paintings, tapestries, silver, porcelain, signet rings and so on, and decided that his nobles must also have their blazons.

The Great Prince Ivan III of Muscovy (*d*1505), was the first Russian ruler to assume the title of Czar (from the Latin Caesar) following his marriage to Sophia (Zoë) Palaeologina, regarded as the heiress of the Byzantine Empire, and with it the double-headed eagle device. Their grandson, Ivan IV, known to history as Ivan the Terrible (*d*1584), initiated the keeping of a register of the nobility, which became known as *The Velvet Book* from its cover. At this period there was no titled nobility apart from the numerous princes descended from cadet branches of the reigning house of Rurik or from the grand ducal house of Gedimin of Lithuania. The other nobles were the boyars who derived their rank from the offices they held.

Peter the Great introduced the titles of count and baron and in 1722 decreed that all officers of the army and navy and functionaries of the civil service above a certain rank thereby acquired hereditary (untitled) nobility and the right to bear arms. About the same time a House of Nobles was established under a Herald Marshal. A peculiarity of the Russian nobility was that all nobles, titled and untitled, were of equal rank and precedence was only determined by the offices they held.

The register of the nobility was kept in the Heraldic Office of the Directing Senate in St Petersburg. An official armorial was begun during the reign of Emperor Paul I (1796–1801) and ten volumes were published.

There are several modern works available on Russian genealogy and heraldry, among them being *La Noblesse de Russie* by Nicolas Ikonnikov (Paris 1938–66, now in process of being re-edited by Prince Dimitri Schakhovskoy), *Dictionnaire de la Noblesse Russe* (Paris 1978) by Patrick de Gmeline, and the excellent and well-illustrated volumes by Jacques Ferrand on the present state of the Russian princely and comital families.

L'Union de la Noblesse Russe is an organization based in Paris and there is also a Russian Nobility Association operating from 971 First Avenue, Apt 20, New York, NY 10022, USA. More recently, since *Glasnost*, a Union of Nobility of Russia is reported to have been established in Moscow, but no details are known.

PART 2

Regalia

The Holy Roman Emperor Leopold II (1790–1792) wearing coronation vestments and the crown of Charlemagne and carrying the
sceptre and orb of Emperor Matthias.

CHAPTER 7

The Origins of Regalia

Crowns, diadems, sceptres, maces and other artefacts worn or carried by monarchs as symbols denoting their status and authority are common to all nations and were known in the earliest civilizations. They were not always, however, constructed from precious materials, the lavish ornamentation and encrustation with jewels being a later development intended to demonstrate the wealth of the ruler and the power and resources of his or her realm.

The White Crown (*Hedjet*) of Upper Egypt, which is depicted on monuments dating from the third millenium BC, was a conical cap with a bulbous top, probably constructed from stiffened linen or buckram, while the Red Crown (*Deshert*) of Lower Egypt was of a rather more curious design but also constructed from simple material. When the Kingdoms of Upper and Lower Egypt were united in the period 3400–3200BC, the crowns were combined into one Double Crown (*Sekhemti*) and the resulting headdress was retained throughout the pharaonic period, although the Egyptian kings continued to wear both the single crowns on ceremonial occasions when assuming the persona of sovereign of either Upper or Lower Egypt. Later, more elaborate crowns or diadems, fashioned from precious metals and jewelled and enamelled, were also worn.

It is a pity that when the modern Kingdom of Egypt was established in 1922, King Fuad I did not adopt a version of the old Double Crown for his heraldic one, but preferred a conventional arched crown of the European type, merely substituting a crescent for the cross surmounting the orb or mound on top. On the other hand, when the new Kingdom of Albania was proclaimed in 1928, King Zog had the good taste to adopt the so-called Helmet of Scanderbeg, Albania's national hero (*d*1467), as the heraldic crown of his dynasty and very impressive it looked.

The Pharaohs' regalia also included ceremonial maces and two sceptres in the form of a crook and a flail, the symbolism of which is obvious. In common with many other ancient monarchies, the Pharaohs were regarded as gods incarnate by their subjects and elaborate ceremonials evolved to mark their coronations, jubilees and funerals, which were celebrated in both the Upper (Southern) and Lower (Northern) Kingdoms

The White, Red and Double Crowns of Egypt.

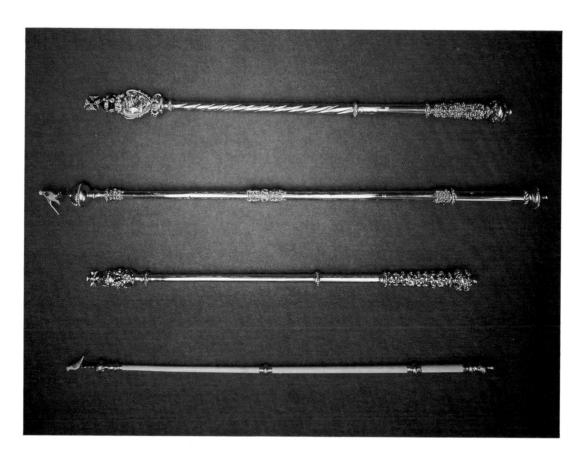

The royal sceptres and rods of England. From the top down: the Royal Sceptre with the Cullinan Diamond set in the head; the Sceptre with the Dove, also known as the Rod of Equity and Mercy; the Queen Consort's Sceptre; the Queen Consort's Ivory Rod. The last two items were made for Mary of Modena's coronation in 1685.

Above: St Edward's Staff (top), part of the English regalia.

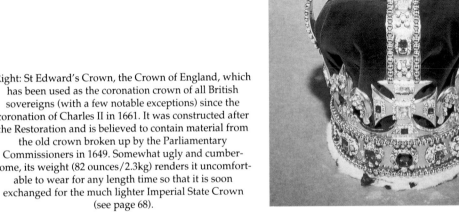

Right: St Edward's Crown, the Crown of England, which has been used as the coronation crown of all British sovereigns (with a few notable exceptions) since the coronation of Charles II in 1661. It was constructed after the Restoration and is believed to contain material from the old crown broken up by the Parliamentary Commissioners in 1649. Somewhat ugly and cumbersome, its weight (82 ounces/2.3kg) renders it uncomfortable to wear for any length time so that it is soon exchanged for the much lighter Imperial State Crown (see page 68).

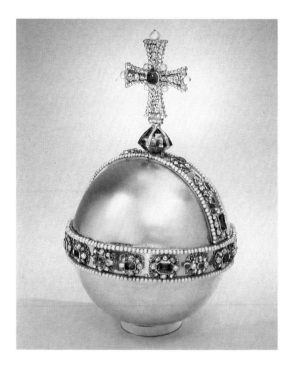

Above: The State Crown and Diadem of Mary of Modena. These two charming little items from the English regalia were made for the coronation of King James II's consort in 1685.

Left: The Orb of England, made originally for the coronation of King Charles II in 1661.

Above left: The Imperial State Crown of England. This crown was originally made for Queen Victoria in 1838 and was used as her actual coronation crown and also as that of King Edward VII in 1902. It was reset in a new frame for King George VI in 1937. The crown contains several famous and historical jewels, including the Black Prince's Ruby (actually a spinel), the Stuart Sapphire, and the second Star of Africa Diamond. It is worn annually at the State Opening of Parliament.

Above right: Queen Elizabeth The Queen Mother's Crown from the English regalia, made for the coronation of King George VI's consort in 1937 and again worn by her, with the arches detached, at the coronation of her daughter Queen Elizabeth II in 1953.

Right: The Prince of Wales's Crown. This very ugly object was made in 1728/9 to be carried on a cushion before Frederick, Prince of Wales, when attending State Openings of Parliament. An equally ugly crown was made for the future King George V to wear at the coronation of his father King Edward VII in 1902, and was also worn by his son the future King Edward VIII in 1911.

The Ampulla and Spoon, the two oldest items of the English regalia, which survived the Parliamentarian destruction and were embellished after the Restoration for Charles II's coronation.

Right: Queen Mary II's Orb, made for the coronation of William and Mary as joint sovereigns of Britain in 1689. It also made an appearance, with the other orb (see page 67), on Queen Victoria's coffin, when it is said to have represented the Empire of India.

Below: The maces of the Serjeants-at-Arms: these items date from the seventeenth century and were formerly kept in the Lord Chamberlain's Office but are now deposited in the Tower of London with the royal regalia.

Above left: The Imperial Crown of India. This crown was made for King George V of Great Britain to wear as Emperor of India when he received the homage of the Indian princes at the Delhi Durbar in 1911, the only occasion on which it has been worn.

Above right: Queen Mary's Crown. This crown was made for the coronation of King George V's consort in 1911. It is of more elegant shape than the crown of her mother-in-law Queen Alexandra. The arches are detachable and Queen Mary wore it without them at the coronation of her son King George VI in 1937.

Left: Queen Victoria's small diamond crown: Queen Victoria had this crown made at her own expense in 1870 and it figures in many of her portraits and photographs. It was deposited in the Tower of London by King George VI in 1937.

The Scottish regalia. The Crown, Sceptre and Sword are the oldest items of regalia in Britain, apart from the Ampulla and Spoon (see page 69). They are kept in the Crown Room of Edinburgh Castle and were presented to HM Queen Elizabeth II at a state service in St Giles's Cathedral when she visited Edinburgh after her coronation in 1953.

with the rites peculiar to each. The king cobra with hood erect also became a powerful symbol of the Egyptian monarchs and adorned the centre of many diadems and headdresses worn by them.

Other ancient kingdoms of the Near East also endowed their rulers with divinity and invested them with crowns and regalia of various distinctive designs, which can be seen on the existing carved stone monuments of Assyria, Babylonia and elsewhere. Some of the crowns depicted have much in common with those worn by the shahs of Iran and emperors of Ethiopia in more modern times, the traditional forms having been passed down through very many generations.

The Parthian kings of the Arsacid Dynasty, who reigned in ancient Persia from about 238BC to AD224, wore crowns which, to judge from their coin portraits, bore a strong resemblance to a good old-fashioned teacosy, sometimes with the addition of horns on the sides. Incidentally, an interesting attribute of the Parthian kings was the royal wart on the forehead, said to be the mark of a true Arsacid and always carefully depicted on the coinage. It is tempting to speculate whether false warts were worn by wartless kings in order to validate their claims to the throne, much as the Pharaohs of Egypt wore false beards (one even being sported by the female ruler Hatshepsut). If so, can they be regarded as an item of regalia? An example of the type of crown worn by Parthian queens is provided by the coin portraits of Queen Musa. This lady began life as a slave girl and was presented to King Phraates IV (38–2BC) by Augustus in exchange for the Roman Eagles (standards), which the Parthians had captured from Crassus and Mark Antony. Musa soon became the King's favourite wife and bore him a son Phraataces, whom she managed to get appointed heir to the throne over the King's other sons. Becoming impatient, however, she and her son murdered the old King and at once contracted an incestuous mother/son marriage which, shocking though it seems, was the Magian custom. Musa appears on several of Phraataces's coins struck at Seleucia. She wears a crown which resembles a three-tiered wedding-cake, a pearl necklace and pendant earrings. The reign of the mother and son was to be of short duration and they appear to have been deposed and murdered about AD4.

The kings of Israel and Judah as recorded in the Bible were the earliest monarchs to be consecrated by being anointed with oil. The oil was contained in a ram's horn and it is noteworthy that very many centuries later the containers for the oil used at the coronations of the kings of Sweden and Norway were fashioned in the shape of a horn constructed from precious metals and studded with gemstones. These seem more pleasingly elegant and certainly more scriptural than the dove or eagle ampullae used in France and England or the pretty 'biscuit barrel' type of container used in Denmark.

Silver drachms of the Parthian Kings Mithradates II (*c*123 – 88BC) and Vonones II (CAD51),
both struck at Ecbatana. That of Mithradates (above left) gives a good impression of the
strange 'teacosy' crown worn by the Parthian monarchs, while that of Vonones shows the
horned ornaments at the sides and the Arsacid royal wart above his left eye.

That the kings of Israel and Judah also wore crowns is known from the account in 2 Samuel I of an Amalekite bringing King Saul's crown to David in about 1056BC, but there is no clue regarding its design or the materials from which it was constructed. Sceptres are also mentioned in the Bible (in Genesis XLIX 10, Psalm XLV 6, and Esther IV 11 for example), but their exact form and symbolism remain a matter of conjecture.

In Europe the ceremonies attendant upon the inauguration or installation of a new sovereign evolved gradually over the course of several centuries, with elements drawn from many different traditions. In ancient Rome victorious generals were awarded triumphs in which they rode through the city crowned with a wreath of golden oakleaves. After the establishment of the Empire various items of regalia were adopted and assumed by successive emperors. The simple oakleaf crown was superseded by the third century AD by a spiked and jewelled diadem, sceptres and, bit by bit, sundry articles of ceremonial attire, including richly decorated buskins or boots. After the adoption of Christianity as the religion of the Empire, Christian symbolism began to creep in and the cross adorned or surmounted most items of the imperial regalia.

The Roman Empire was never, strictly speaking, hereditary, yet it was the ambition of every newly elected emperor to found a dynasty and those who had sons lost no time in associating them in the imperial dignity by conferring the titles of Caesar and Augustus upon them, even though they might be of very tender years. Similarly the title of Augusta was conferred on the wives and daughters of emperors and the portraits of all the members of the imperial family were featured on the coinage. Although the imperial dignity was seldom maintained for more than two generations in the same family, a semblance of legitimacy and continuity was provided by the expedient of persuading the surviving widow or daughter of an emperor to crown and in some cases to marry (usually in name only) his elected successor. In this way the Augusta Pulcheria, sister of the Eastern Emperor Theodosius II (*d*450), married and crowned the able general Marcian on 25 August 450, and five years later her niece Eudoxia, widow of the Western Emperor Valentinian III, set up Petronius Maximus as Emperor at Rome, although he was murdered soon afterwards. Pulcheria predeceased Marcian and when he died there was no Augusta available to crown his elected successor Leo I. Consequently, he was crowned at the Palace of Hebdomon in Constantinople by the Patriarch Anatolius on 7 February 457 and this is the first-recorded Christian coronation, although it is possible that Anatolius had played some part in the coronation of Marcian. From this time onwards it became customary for the Patriarch to crown the emperor and this remained the norm until the fall of the Empire in 1453.

The Roman imperial vestments and regalia became more and more elaborate and their style was copied by the rulers of the medieval Balkan states of Serbia and Bulgaria and also in Russia, where the Muscovite princes claimed to be the heirs of Byzantium following the marriage of the Great Prince Ivan III to Sophia (Zoë) Palaeologina, the niece of the last Byzantine emperor. Many may recall the spectacular coronation scene in Eisenstein's film *Ivan the Terrible*, where the newly crowned young Ivan IV, showered with gold coins, proudly declares: 'Two Romes have fallen; Moscow, the third Rome, stands.'

In western Europe the event which may be said to have initiated the Middle Ages and laid the foundations of the age of chivalry was the Imperial Coronation of Charlemagne at Rome by Pope Leo III on Christmas Day 800. The Pope had determined on this act, an ostensible revival of the Roman Empire in the West, to gain the protection of the man who had become the dominant power in Europe, and used the excuse that the Eastern Empire, whose rulers had hitherto been regarded as the legitimate emperors of Rome, had been usurped by a woman, the Empress Irene. An elaborate charade was staged in St Peter's when the Frankish King, officially unaware of the honour about to be bestowed upon him, entered the church to pray and while kneeling at his devotions was suddenly 'surprised' by the Pope placing a gold crown on his head and announcing that he was 'crowned by God, Great and Peaceful Emperor of the Romans'. Thus began that strange institution, the Holy Roman Empire ('neither Holy, nor Roman, nor an Empire', as has been so aptly said), which was to endure for a thousand years until another self-made emperor, Napoleon, also hailing from the land of the Franks and consecrated by a Pope, presided over its demise.

CHAPTER 8

English Regalia and the Coronation Ceremony

The earliest inauguration ceremonies of kings and tribal leaders throughout Europe took the form of the presentation of the sovereign elect to a gathering of his people, who were asked to signify their consent by acclamation. This done, he was raised shoulder high on a shield so that all might see him and know him. These two elements, now known as The Recognition and The Inthronization, still form part of the coronation rite performed today.

The first reference to a coronation in the modern sense in England is that in the *Anglo-Saxon Chronicle* under the year 787, which tells us that Offa, King of Mercia, who in the course of a reign of thirty years had made himself the overlord of practically the whole of England and was addressed as 'King of the English' by Pope Adrian I, caused his son and heir Ecgfrith to be 'consecrated King'. Offa had succeeded a distant kinsman on the Mercian throne and doubtless thought to consolidate his position by having his only son anointed during his own lifetime, a practice borrowed from the Frankish kings and derived ultimately from the Roman Empire. In Offa's case it was of little avail, for when Ecgfrith succeeded his father in 796 he died childless after a reign of 141 days only and the throne passed to another branch of the Mercian royal family.

The custom of anointing the sovereign with chrism and consecrated oil found its way to western Europe about the middle of the eighth century and was borrowed from the prevailing usage in the Eastern Roman or Byzantine Empire. Following biblical precedent where Samuel anointed David to be King in place of Saul, who had lost God's favour, it was considered a good means by which to confirm and legitimate a new dynasty. To this end, Pepin the Short was anointed and consecrated as King of the Franks after the deposition of the last Merovingian king in 752. At the same time he received the regal ornaments of crown, orb and sceptre. All this was done with papal approval, of course. Nearly fifty years later, as we have seen, Pepin's son Charles (Charlemagne) was crowned Emperor at Rome.

Very little is known of the king-making ceremonies in Saxon England before the ninth century. The kings of the West Saxons (Wessex) were inaugurated at Kingston-on-Thames in the Thames Valley, which derived its name from the ancient stone at which the kings were presented to the people. The stone still stands in the marketplace outside Kingston parish church, but how it came there and when it was first used remain matters of mystery. By tradition Alfred the Great was acclaimed there in 871, as presumably had been his predecessors for many generations. Alfred's son, Edward the Elder, was certainly 'consecrated King' there, as were his four immediate successors, but with the reign of Edgar (959–975) a new and more elaborate rite was initiated.

To digress for a moment, it should be noted that from the time of King Beorhtric of Wessex (786–802), the kings' wives had no share in the regal dignity and were deprived of the title queen (*regina*), being styled instead lady, consort, or companion (indeed our word queen is derived from the old Anglo-Saxon word *cwen*, meaning companion or wife). The reason for this is that Beorhtric was accidentally poisoned by his wife Eadburh, a daughter of King Offa of Mercia, and this aroused such horror among the people that it was decreed that no woman ever be honoured as queen again. This rule held good with respect to the wife of King Egbert and the first wife of King Ethelwulf, but when the latter married his second wife, Judith, daughter of Charles the Bald, King of the Franks, on Ethelwulf's return journey from his pilgrimage to Rome in 856, she was at the same time 'consecrated Queen'. It was on this same pilgrimage to Rome that Ethelwulf's youngest son Alfred, who accompanied him, was anointed by Pope Leo IV, probably as part of the rite of confirmation, although Alfred's biographer Asser saw it as a consecration to future kingship, an eventuality which could hardly have been contemplated as Alfred had at least three elder brothers living.

When Alfred's great-grandson Edgar succeeded to the throne on the death of his brother Edwy in 959, it seems reasonable to suppose that he was consecrated at Kingston like his predecessors, although there is no specific mention of the act. In 973, however, Dunstan, Archbishop of Canterbury, the most powerful and influential man in the realm, determined on holding a far more impressive ceremony. The 'order' which he drew up was derived from that used at the coronations of the Frankish kings and contains most of the elements common to all subsequent coronations. The ceremony took place at Bath Abbey on Whit Sunday 11 May 973 and Edgar's second wife Elfrida was anointed and crowned with him, finally ending the restrictions imposed on the king's wife to bar her from a share in his dignity. The proceedings opened with a procession on foot to the church. The King was flanked by two bishops and surrounded by other high-ranking ecclesiastics. He wore his crown (an indication that he had already been crowned previously at Kingston), but removed it before the high altar. He then prostrated himself while Dunstan and the other clergy sang the *Te Deum*. This ended, his supporting bishops raised him up and Dunstan administered a threefold oath to the King: to guard the church of God, to forbid violence and wrong, and to keep justice, judgement and mercy. Prayers followed and Edgar was then anointed while the choir sang the antiphon telling of Zadok the priest and Nathan the prophet anointing Solomon King (still sung at this point of the service and since the coronation of George II to the exhilarating music of Handel). The King was then invested with a ring, girt with a sword and crowned. He also received the sceptre and the rod. Queen Elfrida was then crowned and the mass proceeded to its end. A coronation banquet followed with the King and Queen presiding in different halls of the palace.

From the account it can be seen that the royal regalia then consisted of crown, sceptre, rod, ring and sword, and the queen's regalia of crown and ring. There is no mention of an orb or mound at this period, but it was probably introduced into the regalia soon after and certainly by the reign of Edward the Confessor (1042–1066), who is depicted holding one on his great seal.

The crown of coronation only became known as St Edward's Crown from the time of King Edward I (1272–1307), and there are also references to 'the coat of St Edward' and 'the royal ornaments of St Edward'. It is supposed that these artefacts were removed from the tomb of St Edward (Edward the Confessor) when it was opened and his body re-enshrined by King Henry III. They were regarded as so sacred that they were used as the chief instruments of coronation for Edward I and all his successors down to Charles I, although they must have been decidedly shoddy after being buried with the Confessor for two hundred years. Between coronations the regalia remained in the custody of Westminster Abbey. From the Norman Conquest at least, each king and queen had his or her own crown made and they may be considered the forerunners of the State Crowns worn on the return from the Abbey and subsequently at State Openings of Parliament. The exact form of some of these early crowns may be deduced from monumental effigies, coins and illuminated manuscripts. A rather fanciful set of replicas of these early and now for-ever lost regalia was made some time before the 1937 coronation and was once in the possession of a Mr Max Berman (but if it still exists its where-abouts is unknown to the author).

There are only two items in the present regalia which predate the reign of Charles II, the Ampulla and the Anointing Spoon. The Ampulla, of solid gold, is in the form of an eagle, the head of which unscrews to allow it to be filled with the holy oil for the sovereign's anointing, which is then poured through the beak into the Anointing Spoon. The Ampulla is of late-fourteenth-century workmanship and was used at the coronation of King Henry IV (1399). There are many legends concerning the origin of this vessel or its precursor, notably that it had been given to Thomas à Becket by the Virgin Mary but was then lost or hidden in Poitiers for a number of years until found by the Black Prince, was again mislaid so that it was not used for the consecration of Richard II, only to emerge again for that of Henry IV. This seems an obvious piece of Lancastrian propaganda concocted to justify the usurping Henry's right to the throne. The Anointing Spoon, of silver gilt, is of an earlier date than the Ampulla, being of late-twelfth-century style. These two items do not appear on the lists enumerating the articles removed from Westminster Abbey and taken to the Tower of London for destruction by the Parliamentary Commissioners, so it is presumed that they were kept apart from the rest of the regalia, probably with the Abbey plate, and thus escaped notice. They were recovered for use at Charles II's coronation and both received a certain amount of embellishment, the eagle being realistically engraved to represent feathers and the spoon being chased in typical seventeenth-century style.

An interesting item of the English regalia is St Edward's Staff. The walking-staff of Edward the Confessor, probably taken from his tomb, is mentioned in an inventory of 1606 as 'a long Scepter with a Pike of Steele in the bottome', and this description served as a model when the new set of regalia was made for Charles II's coronation. However, its exact function had been forgotten and it was merely carried before the sovereign with the other regalia and then placed on the altar. From sundry references it would appear that the Staff was handed to the later medieval kings by the Abbot of Westminster when they visited the Abbey in State, much in the same way as the Lord Mayor of London surrenders the city sword when the monarch makes official visits to the city. It would be a pleasing innovation at future coronations if the Dean of Westminster handed St Edward's Staff to the sovereign on his or her arrival at the Abbey and it was retained and used as a walking-staff during the procession into the church and then returned to the Dean to be placed on the altar.

As already stated, Parliament, intent on abolishing the monarchy for good, ordered the regalia to be broken up in 1649. The items were taken from Westminster Abbey to the Tower of London, where they were listed, valued and then broken up. The gold from most items was ordered to be delivered to the Mint and the jewels were sold to various private jewellers. The inventory, now in the British Library, begins as follows:

Queen Ediths Crowne formerly thought to be of Massy Gold, but upon tryale found to be of Silver Gilt, Enriched with Garnetts, foule Pearls, Saphyrs & Some odd Stones weighing 50:oz$^{1}/_{2}$ ...

This item was valued at £16. The next item, 'King Elfreds Crowne of Gold wyreworke Sett with Slight Stones and two little Bells', was valued more highly, at £248.10.0. This, it is thought, was St Edward's Crown which, it was believed, had previously been that of Alfred the Great. The inventory goes on to list other items, the total valuation amounting to £2,647.18.4, a ludicrously small sum even for those days.

Eleven years after the breakup of the regalia, King Charles II was restored to the throne and it became necessary to make a new set of regalia for his coronation. As we have seen, the Ampulla and Anointing Spoon had survived and it is believed that some of the gold from the old St Edward's Crown was recovered and incorporated into the new one. Several jewels with which the old regalia had been set were also recovered, notably the large spinel known as 'The Black Prince's Ruby', which was set in the centre of the State Crown. Charles II was unmarried when he was crowned, so no queen's regalia were required until the following reign, when James II's queen, Mary of Modena, was crowned with her husband. A diadem, two crowns, two sceptres and a ring were provided, and set with hired stones. For the coronation of William and Mary as joint sovereigns in 1689 a second orb had to be provided for the Queen. A detailed list of the existing English regalia will be found in Appendix 2.

As might be expected, coronations have not always run smoothly and with the seemingly effortless precision which is the hallmark of all royal ceremonies today. Almost every one has been the occasion of some untoward incident to cause embarrassment to some of the individuals involved and amusement to others.

The coronation of William the Conqueror on Christmas Day 1066 was the scene of a riot when the King's Norman followers mistook the Saxon acclamation of the newly crowned sovereign as an incitement to revolt and fell upon the crowds outside the Abbey, putting many to the sword and setting fire to some of the wood and wattle buildings in the neighbourhood. Order was restored by the King himself on emerging from the Abbey.

At the coronation of King Henry I's second wife, Adeliza of Louvain, in 1122, the King, who had himself been crowned many years before, entered the Abbey wearing his crown and took his seat on his throne to witness his consort's crowning. The near-senile Archbishop of Canterbury, Ralph d'Escures, seeing him and imagining that his right to crown the sovereign had been infringed, flew into a rage and either snatched the crown from the startled King's head or knocked it off with his pastoral staff. Matters were explained to him and, after replacing the crown on Henry's head, he proceeded to the coronation of the Queen.

Henry II copied the custom of the French court by having his eldest surviving son and heir, Henry, crowned in his own lifetime. There were

The Crown wherwith the Queen was Crowned.

V

This engraving, taken from Sandford's *Coronation of James II*, represents the Coronation Crown made for Mary of Modena in 1685. It bears a close resemblance to St Edward's Crown (see page 66).

in fact two ceremonies, as the younger Henry's father-in-law, Louis VII of France, objected to the fact that his daughter had not been crowned with her husband and demanded that the matter should be rectified. As it happened, Henry died before his father.

From the coronation of Edward II (1307), the coronation 'order' was gathered into a definitive form in the *Liber Regalis*, which continued in use until the coronation of Charles II, being rather barbarously rendered into English for that of James I. In 1685 King James II charged Sancroft, the Archbishop of Canterbury, to 'abbridge (as much as conveniently might be) the extreme length' of the order. Sancroft was no liturgiologist and the result was not an altogether happy one. The order was further revised for the coronation of William and Mary by Henry Compton, Bishop of London, who officiated in Sancroft's place, that prelate having scruples about crowning another in James II's lifetime. A feature unique to this coronation, apart from the fact that it was a joint one, was the inclusion of a prayer for the consecration of the anointing oil in the course of the service, whereas both before and since that rite has always been performed privately before the main service.

As the ceremonial involved in coronations became more elaborate, the nobility began to play a role in the proceedings by having certain duties assigned to them or by performing specific offices by which they held tenure of their lands or manors. It thus became necessary before each coronation to set up a Court of Claims, presided over by the Lord Chancellor, to consider the claims put forward by those who considered it their right to perform these offices or services. The Lord High Steward, for example, has the right to bear St Edward's Crown in the procession into the Abbey and other peers claim the right to bear different items of the regalia. The most picturesque claims in medieval times, however, were those which were attached to lordships of certain manors, most of which have now lapsed or been commuted since the abolition of the Coronation Banquet after 1821. Among these may be mentioned the lordship of the manor of Liston in Essex, held on condition of providing five wafers of fine flour to place before the King at dinner; the lordship of the manor of Heydon, also in Essex, held by the duty of holding the basin, ewer and towel for the King to wash his hands before dinner and receiving the towel as his fee; the lordship of the manor of Addington in Sussex held by providing 'one mess in an earthen pot' called *maupygernon*. This last appears to have originated when the tenure of the manor was granted to one Bartholomew de Cheney, Henry I's cook, and the 'mess' was a concoction of 'almond milk, brawn of capons, sugar and spices, and chickens parboiled and chopped' – a mess indeed. Another manor (in Kent) was held by the service of presenting the King with three maple cups on his coronation day. The Barons of the Cinque Ports claimed the right to carry the canopies over the King and Queen in the coronation procession and to receive them afterwards as their fee. Some of the bells from the canopies used at James II's coronation may be seen in Winchelsea Museum. Although still represented at coronations, the Barons now have no duties to perform as the canopy is now held over the sovereign by four Knights of the Garter, and only for his or her anointing, and over a Queen Consort by four Duchesses.

Since the coronation of Edward II, every sovereign, with the exceptions of Mary I and Mary II, has been crowned seated on the Coronation Chair which was constructed to the order of King Edward I to contain beneath its seat the Stone of Destiny, which he had carried off from Scotland in 1296. Mary I was crowned in a chair sent to her by the Pope and for Mary II, as joint sovereign, a smaller-sized replica of the Coronation Chair was made. The Stone of Destiny was the ancient Coronation Stone of the Scottish kings, allegedly brought from Ireland by Fergus Mor Mac Erc and said to be the very stone on which Jacob rested his head at Bethel when he had his dream of angels ascending and descending a ladder into heaven. However, the opinion of geologists is that it is of Scottish origin and quarried from one of the sandstone districts between the coast of Argyle and the mouths of the Tay or Forth. Be this as it may, Edward I caused one Master Walter to construct a handsome oak chair to contain the stone and it still stands in Westminster Abbey near the Confessor's shrine, whence it is moved into the sanctuary for each coronation. It has become decidedly worse for wear over the years, having suffered much from the depredations of amateur woodcarvers intent on leaving their own initials upon its surface. The only occasion on which it left the Abbey was for the installation of Oliver Cromwell as Lord Protector in Westminster Hall in 1653 and the only other occasion on which it has been used apart from a coronation was when Queen Victoria sat in it for her Golden Jubilee service at the Abbey in 1887. In 1951 the Coronation Stone was stolen from beneath the chair by Scottish Nationalists, causing much distress to King George VI, but happily it was recovered undamaged a few months later.

The 'Form and Order' which has been followed for all coronations since that of William IV and Queen Adelaide in 1831, is essentially the same as that used for the coronation of King Edgar in 973. It falls into nineteen sections:

    I The Preparation
    II The Entrance into the Church
    III The Recognition
    IV The Litany (now sung by the Abbey clergy before the
       Preparation)

V The Beginning of the Communion Service
VI The Sermon (now omitted)
VII The Oath
VIII The Anointing
IX The Presenting of the Spurs and Sword, and the Girding and Oblation of the said Sword
X The Investing with the Armilla and Imperial Mantle, and the Delivery of the Orb
XI The Investiture per Annulum et Baculum
XII The Putting on of the Crown
XIII The Presenting of the Holy Bible
XIV The Benedictions
XV The Inthronization
XVI The Homage
XVII The Queen's Coronation
XVIII The Communion
XIX The Recess

The coronation in 1661 of King Charles II, the first to make use of the new regalia, was also the last occasion on which the monarch went in procession from the Tower of London to Westminster on the coronation eve. The event was witnessed by the diarist John Evelyn, who described it as follows:

> This magnificent traine on horseback, as rich as embroidery, velvet, cloth of gold and silver, and jewells, could make them and their pransing horses, proceed'd thro' the streetes strew'd with flowers, houses hung with rich tapessry, windoes and balconies full of ladies; the London Militia lining the ways, and the severall Companies with their banners and loud musiq rank'd in their orders; the fountaines running wine, bells ringing, with speeches made at the severall triumphal arches; at that of the Temple Barr (neere which I stood) the Lord Maior was receiv'd by the Bayliff of Westminster, who in a scarlet robe made a speech. Thence with joyful acclamations his Majestie passed to Whitehall. Bonfires at night.

The next morning Evelyn was in the Abbey to witness the actual coronation. The King travelled the short distance from Whitehall to Westminster by water, and Evelyn takes up the tale:

> When his Majestie was enter'd, the Deane and Prebendaries brought all the regalia, and deliver'd them to severall Noblemen to beare before the King, who met them at the west doore of the Church

singing an anthem, to the Quire. Then came the Peers in their robes, and coronets in their hands, til his Majestie was plac'd in a throne elevated before the altar. Then the Bishop of London (the Archbishop of Canterbury being sick) went to every side of throne to present the King to the People, asking if they would have him for their King and do him homage; at this they shouted 4 times God save King Charles the Second! Then an anthem was sung. Then his Majestie attended by 3 Bishops went up to the altar, and he offer'd a pall and a pound of gold. Afterwards he sate downe in another chaire during the sermon, which was preach'd by Dr. Morley then Bishop of Worcester. After sermon the King tooke his oath before the altar to maintain the Religion, Magna Charta, and Laws of the Land. The hymn Veni S. Sp. follow'd, and then the Litany by 2 Bishops. Then the Archbishop of Canterbury, present but much indispos'd and weake, said Lift up your hearts; at which the King rose up and put off his robes and upper garments, and was in a waistcoate so opened in divers places that the Archb'p might commodiously anoint him, first in the palmes of his hands, when an anthem was sung and a prayer read; then his breast and twixt the shoulders, bending of both armes, and lastly on the crowne of the head, with apposite hymns and prayers at each anoynting; this don, the Deane clos'd and button'd up the wastcoate. Then was a coyfe put on, and the cobbium, syndon, or dalmatic, and over this a supertunic of cloth of gold, with buskins and sandals of the same, spurrs, and the sword, a prayer being first said over it by the Archbishop on the altar before t'was girt on by the Lord Chamberlaine. Then the armill, mantle, &c. Then the Archbishop plac'd the crowne imperial on the altar pray'd over it, and set it on his Majesties head, at which all the Peers put on their coronets. Anthems and rare musiq with lutes, viols, trumpets, organs, and voices, were then heard, and the Archbishop put a ring on his Majesties finger. The King next offer'd his sword on the altar, which being redeemed was drawn and borne before him. Then the Archbishop deliver'd him the sceptre with the dove in one hand, and in the other the sceptre with the globe. Then the King kneeling, the Archbishop pronounc'd the blessing. The King then ascending againe his Royal Throne, whilst Te Deum was singing, all the Peeres did their homage, by every one touching his crowne. The Archbishop and rest of the Bishops first kissing the King; who receiv'd the holy sacrament, and so disrob'd, yet with the crowne imperial on his head, and accompanied with all the Nobility in the former order, he went on foote upon blew cloth, which was spread and reach'd from the West dore of the Abby to Westminster stayres, when he tooke water in a triumphal barge to Whitehall, where was extraordinary feasting.

It seems strange that Evelyn, usually very well informed, was under the impression that the coronation banquet was held at Whitehall instead of Westminster Hall. His fellow diarist Samuel Pepys also recorded the events and was just as impressed as Evelyn had been by the Knights of the Bath ('a brave sight of itself') and the two men representing the Dukes of Normandy and Aquitaine. As a 'gatecrasher' his view in the Abbey was somewhat restricted, but after the coronation he made his way to Westminster Hall:

> ... where it was very fine with hangings and scaffolds one upon another full of brave ladies; and my wife in one little one, on the right hand. Here I staid walking up and down, and at last upon one of the side stalls I stood and saw the King come in with all the persons (but the soldiers) that were yesterday in the cavalcade; and a most pleasant sight it was to see them in their several robes. And the King came in with his crown on, and his sceptre in his hand, under a canopy borne up by six silver staves, carried by Barons of the Cinque Ports, and little bells at every end. And after a long time, he got up to the farther end, and all set themselves down at their several tables; and that was also a brave sight: and the King's first course carried up by the Knights of the Bath. And many fine ceremonies there was of the Heralds leading up people before him, and bowing; and my Lord of Albemarle's going to the kitchin and eat a bit of the first dish that was to go to the King's table. But, above all, was these three Lords, Northumberland, and Suffolk, and the Duke of Ormond, coming before the courses on horseback, and staying so all dinner-time, and at last to bring up the King's Champion, all in armour on horseback, with his spear and targett carried before him. And a Herald proclaims 'That if any dare deny Charles Stewart to be lawful King of England, here was a Champion that would fight with him;' and with these words, the Champion flings down his gauntlet, and all this he do three times in his going up towards the King's table. At last when he is come, the King drinks to him, and then sends him the cup which is of gold, and he drinks its off, and then rides back again with the cup in his hand.

At the next coronation, that of James II and Mary of Modena, Pepys was himself one of the Barons of the Cinque Ports, but having by then long ceased to keep his diary, he has left no account of the proceedings, while Evelyn noted tersely, 'The solemnity was magnificent, as is set forth in print', adding 'Having been present at the late King's Coronation, I was not ambitious of seeing this ceremonie'. A month later, on 21 May 1685, Evelyn 'din'd at my Lord Privy Seal's with Sir William Dugdale, Garter

HM Queen Elizabeth II processing through the Royal Gallery to the House of Lords for her first State Opening of Parliament on 4 November 1952. She is wearing her parliamentary robe of crimson velvet and the collar of the Order of the Garter. As her coronation had not yet taken place, she did not wear the Imperial State Crown but retained the diamond diadem of King George IV which she had worn on her drive from Buckingham Palace. The Queen and Prince Philip are preceded by Field Marshal Earl Alexander of Tunis bearing the Sword of State, and wearing his parliamentary robes and the collar of the Order of the Garter over Field Marshal's uniform.

King of Armes, author of the Monasticon and other learned works: he told me he was 82 yeares of age, and had his sight and memory perfect. There was shewn a draught of the exact shape and dimensions of the Crowne the Queene had been crowned withall, together with the jewells and pearls; their weight and value, which amounted to £100,658 sterling, attested at the foote of the paper by the jeweller and goldsmith who sett them'.

Evelyn lived to see two more coronations. At that of William and Mary on 11 April 1689, he 'saw the Procession to and from the Abby Church of Westminster, with the greate Feast in Westminster Hall', and noted that 'Much of the splendor of the proceeding was abated by the absence of divers who should have contributed to it, there being but five Bishops, foure Judges (no more being yet sworn), and severall noblemen and greate ladys wanting; the feast, however, was magnificent'. Queen Anne's coronation in 1702 was not noted by Evelyn.

The coronation of King George I presented a problem because of the King's rudimentary knowledge of English. It was solved by conducting the service in Latin, a language which had not been employed in Church of England worship since the Reformation and at a coronation since that of Queen Elizabeth I.

The coronations of George II and George III were both enhanced by the fact that their consorts were crowned with them. George III's coronation, furthermore, was the last at which the Dukes of Normandy and Aquitaine were personated. Two actors were engaged to play the roles and their posturing and histrionic gestures aroused a great deal of wry amusement among the spectactors. After the title of King of France was dropped from the royal style in 1801, it was no longer deemed necessary for the two great peers of France to be personated at coronations.

George IV, always a great showman, was determined that his coronation in 1821 should be the most magnificent ever seen. A new State Crown was made and used as the actual coronation crown in preference to St Edward's Crown, which was nevertheless carried in the procession and placed on the altar with the rest of the regalia. Instead of wearing the Cap of Maintenance (see Glossary) on his journey to the Abbey in accordance with custom, the King wore a diadem set with diamonds, which was later adapted for Queen Victoria and also for the present Queen, who not only wore it on her coronation day but also wears it on the drive to and from the State Opening of Parliament every year. The coronation vestments and other royal robes, as well as the robes of the peers and peeresses, were all redesigned and appear to have been extremely elegant judging from contemporary engravings and surviving examples. The cloth-of-gold Dalmatic Robe and Imperial Mantle made for George IV were subsequently also used by King George V (1911), King George VI (1937), and HM Queen Elizabeth II (1953), and are still in excellent condition.

George IV's coronation was only marred by the pathetic attempts made by his estranged wife Queen Caroline, for whose coronation no provision had been made, to gain entry to the Abbey and her demand to be crowned either with him or separately on a later date. Frustrated in her design, the poor Queen, who was already ailing, fell desperately ill and died within a month.

So much money had been expended on George IV's coronation that the government decreed that of his brother and successor William IV and his consort should be drastically curtailed and there was even a motion to abolish the ceremony altogether as it had been in several European countries. The procession on foot between Westminster Hall and the Abbey and the coronation banquet were done away with and so many economies were effected that the whole proceedings were lampooned in the press as the 'half-crownation'. It had long been the custom to hire the

HM Queen Elizabeth II awaiting the homage of her peers after being 'lifted' on to her throne at her coronation in Westminster Abbey on 2 June 1953. The Queen is clad in the cloth of gold Imperial Mantle and Supertunica of King George IV and is wearing St Edward's Crown. She holds the Royal Sceptre and the Sceptre with the Dove, but unfortunately the Armills or bracelets are not visible in this picture. The Bishops of Durham and Bath and Wells 'support' the Queen on either side and the throne is surrounded by peers of different degrees wearing their coronets and coronation robes or (as in the case of Viscount Portal) Garter robes. The Marquess of Salisbury is bearing the Sword of State.

The crown frame of Queen Adelaide made
for her coronation in 1831. It was set with
the Queen's own jewels as she disliked the
idea of using hired jewels in accordance
with established custom.

gems with which the queen consort's crown was set, but Queen Adelaide so much disliked the idea of being crowned with hired jewels that she provided items from her own personal jewellery to be set in her pretty little crown, the frame of which may be seen today in the Museum of London. For her journey to Westminster and the first part of the service she wore the diadem of Mary of Modena, being the last queen consort to do so. For some reason, Queen Alexandra, Queen Mary, and Queen Elizabeth did not choose to do the same; but may we hope that this beautiful little diadem may one day grace the brow of our present Princess of Wales when she goes to her crowning as the consort of King Charles III?

Queen Victoria's coronation provoked much interest, not only because she was the first queen regnant since Anne over a hundred years before, but also on account of her youth. At nineteen she was the youngest

Queen Alexandra's Crown made for her coronation in 1902. Originally set with diamonds, it was
later reset with paste and presented to the
London Museum (now the Museum of London)
by the Queen.

monarch to have been crowned since Edward VI. The Queen herself
wrote an interesting account of her coronation day in her diary, part of
which is reproduced here:

> I reached the Abbey amid deafening cheers at a little after half-past
> eleven; I first went into a robing-room quite close to the entrance
> where I found my eight train-bearers . . . all dressed alike and
> beautifully in white satin and silver tissue with wreaths of silver
> corn-ears in front, and a small one of pink roses round the plait
> behind, and pink roses in the trimming of the dresses.
>
> After putting on my mantle, and the young ladies having properly
> got hold of it and Lord Conyngham holding the end of it, I left the
> robing-room and the Procession began . . . The sight was splendid; the

bank of Peeresses quite beautiful all in their robes, and the Peers on the other side. My young train-bearers were always near me, and helped me whenever I wanted anything. The Bishop of Durham stood on the side near me, but he was, as Lord Melbourne told me, remarkably *maladroit*, and never could tell me what was to take place. At the beginning of the Anthem . . . I retired to St. Edward's Chapel, a dark small place immediately behind the Altar, with my ladies and train-bearers – took off my crimson robe and kirtle, and put on the supertunica of cloth of gold, also in the shape of a kirtle, which was put over a singular sort of little gown of linen trimmed with lace; I also took off my circlet of diamonds and then proceeded bare-headed into the Abbey; I was then seated upon St Edward's chair, where the Dalmatic robe was clasped round me by the Lord Great Chamberlain. Then followed all the various things; and last . . . the Crown being placed on my head – which was, I must own, a most beautiful impressive moment; *all* the Peers and Peeresses put on their coronets at the same instant.

My excellent Lord Melbourne, who stood very close to me throughout the whole ceremony, was *completely* overcome at this moment, and very much affected; he gave me *such* a kind, and I may say *fatherly* look. The shouts, which were very great, the drums, the trumpets, the firing of the guns, all at the same instant, rendered the spectacle most imposing.

The Enthronisation and the Homage of, first, all the Bishops, and then my Uncles, and lastly of all the Peers, in their respective order was very fine. The Duke of Norfolk (holding for me the Sceptre with a Cross) with Lord Melbourne stood close to me on my right, and the Duke of Richmond with the other Sceptre on my left, etc., etc. All my train-bearers, etc., standing behind the Throne. Poor old Lord Rolle, who is 82, and dreadfully infirm, in attempting to ascend the steps fell and rolled quite down, but was not the least hurt; when he attempted to re-ascend them I got up and advanced to the end of the steps, in order to prevent another fall. When Lord Melbourne's turn to do Homage came, there was loud cheering; they also cheered Lord Grey and the Duke of Wellington; it's a pretty ceremony; they first all touch the Crown, and then kiss my hand . . . After the Homage was concluded I left the Throne, took off my Crown and received the Sacrament; I then put on my Crown again, and re-ascended the Throne, leaning on Lord Melbourne's arm. At the commencement of the Anthem I descended from the Throne, and went into St Edward's Chapel with my Ladies, Train-bearers, and Lord Willoughby, where I took off the Dalmatic robe, supertunica, etc., and put on the Purple Velvet Kirtle and Mantle, and proceeded again to the Throne, which I ascended leaning on Lord Melbourne's hand . . .

At about half-past four I re-entered my carriage, the Crown on my head, and the Sceptre and Orb in my hands, and we proceeded the same way as we came – the crowds if possible having increased. The enthusiasm, affection, and loyalty were really touching, and I shall ever remember this day as the *Proudest* of my life! I came home at a little after six, really *not* feeling tired.

Victoria's reign was so long that when the time came for her son and successor King Edward VII and his consort Alexandra to be crowned in 1902, there were very few left who had been present when the old Queen had been crowned in 1838. One exception was Grand Duchess Augusta of Mecklenburg-Strelitz, born Princess Augusta of Cambridge, Victoria's first cousin, who was able to proffer much advice to her niece May, Princess of Wales, later to become Queen Mary, the consort of King George V. The Grand Duchess was present at the coronation of 1902 and there is a photograph of her in her coronation robes and coronet in the Royal Archives at Windsor. Edward VII's coronation was originally planned to take place on 26 June 1902, but a few days before that he was struck down with acute appendicitis and underwent an operation from which he recovered so speedily that the ceremony, somewhat curtailed to spare the convalescent King from too much fatigue, was held on 9 August 1902 (incidentally, the only coronation to take place on a Saturday).

For the coronations of King George V, King George VI and Queen Elizabeth II, annexes were built outside the west door of the Abbey to allow for the marshalling of the processions and the transfer of the regalia from the Dean and Chapter of Westminster to the peers appointed to carry them. Until George IV's coronation these proceedings had taken place in Westminster Hall, while at those of William IV, Victoria and Edward VII the marshalling was contrived in the restricted space of the west end of the Abbey and the Jerusalem Chamber.

The coronation of King George V was the first at which a strictly limited number of photographs was allowed to be taken inside the Abbey; that of King George VI was broadcast and filmed; and that of Queen Elizabeth II was broadcast, filmed and televised, bringing the picturesque ceremonial to a wider audience than ever known previously and providing a valuable record for the future.

CHAPTER 9

Non-royal Regalia

Regalia, despite the implications of the name, are not confined to royalty. Kings of arms, heralds, pursuivants, peers and peeresses, judges, chancellors, mayors and other civic dignitaries, all make use of certain items of regalia, as do Freemasons and members of similar fraternities.

Among the most interesting such items are the crowns worn at coronations by the kings of arms. These are of silver gilt and are composed of a circlet surmounted by acanthus leaves. At coronations they are assumed at the moment when the sovereign is crowned and the peers put on their coronets. The kings of arms also wear gold 'Collars of SS' (see below) and the heralds silver ones. The tabards worn by the kings of arms are embroidered on silk velvet, those of heralds on satin, and those of pursuivants on figured silk damask. In Scotland the crown of the Lord Lyon king of arms is modelled on the Crown of Scotland.

Coronets are worn by princes and princesses of the blood royal and by peers and peeresses. There are several varieties of coronet for members of the royal family, with subtle differences only apparent on close examination. Although these are adhered to heraldically, they have not always been used correctly in actual fact. There are photographs of princesses wearing coronets to which, strictly speaking, they were not entitled, the coronets allotted to the grandchildren of a sovereign in the male line being different from those appropriate to the children of a sovereign, for example.

The coronets appropriate to the five degrees of the peerage – duke, marquess, earl, viscount and baron – are described in the Glossary. Coronets were first allotted to viscounts by Queen Elizabeth I and to barons by King Charles II. Although used heraldically, they are only actually worn at coronations where the peers assume theirs at the moment the King is crowned and the peeresses at the moment the Queen Consort is crowned. On occasion, coronets also make a ceremonial appearance at peers' funerals. The coronet of the 16th Duke of Norfolk was carried at his funeral in 1975, and that of the 15th Earl of Huntingdon was placed on his coffin in 1990.

The Collar of SS, already mentioned, is an item of regalia whose origin seems to be wrapped in mystery. It dates at least from the time of Henry IV, who used an SS badge, and the letters are said to represent his personal motto, 'Sovereygne'. Other sources say the letters stand for *seneschallus* (steward), or for *Sanctus Spiritus* (the Holy Spirit). Henry V granted the right to wear a Collar of ss to several officials after the battle of Agincourt in 1415 and a portrait of Henry VI shows him wearing a collar composed of single Ss. Henry VII gave the collar a different form by alternating the ss with portcullises and adding a Tudor rose or portcullis pendant. Henry VIII prescribed its use to knights and it was worn by such dignitaries as the Lord Chancellor, the Lord High Steward, the Lord Chief Justice and the Lord Mayor of London. Today it is worn by the kings of arms and heralds, as already stated, the Lord Chief Justice, the Lord Mayor of London and the Serjeants-at-Arms, whose duty it is to carry the mace.

Collars, or chains as they are more commonly called, have long formed part of the regalia or insignia of mayors of cities and towns, that of Kingston-on-Hull dating from 1564. Most of the earlier ones are of a simple type, but from the middle of the nineteenth century they began to be more elaborate and, as St John Hope wrote in his delightfully detailed book *Heraldry for Craftsmen and Designers*, 'appalling creations many of them are, with rows of tablet links, and armorial pendants as large as saucers'. Chains are also worn by mayors' wives, and their use is now extended to deputy mayors and mayoresses as well. Holders of office in guilds and livery companies also wear chains with the coat of arms of the company on a badge suspended from them.

Maces are important items of regalia, used as symbols of judicial or civic authority. Their usual form is a shaft supporting a bulbous head surmounted by a representation of the Imperial Crown. Originally a weapon wielded in battle by members of the clergy, whose holy orders forbade the shedding of blood by the sword but deemed it all right to clobber their enemies to death with a blunt instrument, the mace was relegated to a purely ceremonial use by the end of the fourteenth century. The House of Commons mace was made by Thomas Maundy in 1649 and remodelled with royal symbols after the Restoration in 1660. The House of Lords possesses two maces, the earlier dating from the reign of William III. Eight large maces of the serjeants-at-arms are kept with the regalia in the Tower of London; two date from the reign of Charles II, two from that of James II, three from that of William and Mary, and one from that of Queen Anne (to which the cypher of George I has been added). Ceremonial maces were also used in several states in the American colonies and are still preserved as treasured relics of the past.

Some mention should be made of the so-called regalia used by the Freemasons, Oddfellows, and other fraternal societies in their ceremonies. These consist of collars, cuffs and aprons constructed from fabrics and leathers and embellished with metal ornaments. The holders of various offices in these bodies are usually distinguished by a 'jewel', which takes the form of an enamelled medal.

CHAPTER 10

Royal Regalia and Coronations of the World

Although the British regalia are probably the fullest set in the world, they are far from being the most beautiful or even the most valuable.

The oldest existing crowns in Europe are those of the kings of the Visigoths in Spain, who were in the habit of presenting them as votive offerings to Toledo Cathedral, where several of them are still to be seen hanging. They take the form of circlets of gold, studded with uncut gems, and it is by no means certain that they were ever worn, it being possible that they were manufactured solely for votive purposes, much as crowns for statues of the Virgin were made in later times. Another splendid Visigothic crown is that of King Recceswinth (653–672), which was found hidden in a well by a farmer and his wife in 1858. They sold it to Queen Isabel II's jeweller for a paltry sum and he smuggled it out of the country and sold it to the French government. It was exhibited in the Musée de Cluny in Paris until 1940, when General Franco negotiated its return to Spain with Marshal Pétain, the Vichy head of state. Since then it has been in the Archaeological Museum in Madrid. The crown is similar to those described and has the King's name spelt out in letters pendant from the rim.

In later times the kings of Aragon and of Navarre were crowned, but those of Castile were not, and when Spain became united into one kingdom it was the custom of Castile which was followed. There was a symbolic set of regalia, however, and when Napoleon invaded Spain, King Carlos IV had his crown and other items walled up in the palace. Unfortunately, the exact location was forgotten and they have never been recovered. A symbolic crown made in 1775 for use at royal funerals was used for accession oath-takings in the Cortes from the time of Queen Isabel II, together with a sceptre dating from the seventeenth century. The crown was packed away after King Alfonso XIII left the country in 1931 and found in a box in the basement of the palace just in time to be displayed when King Juan Carlos I took the oath in the Cortes in November 1975. The crown was also placed on King Alfonso XIII's coffin when he

The Byzantine Emperor Nicephorus III Botaniates (1078–1081), seated in state
wearing his imperial robes, buskins and an open crown, as depicted in a contemporary
manuscript. Note the convention whereby the Emperor's attendants, as lesser
mortals, are drawn on a small scale.

The Byzantine Emperor John VI Cantacuzene (1347–1354) seated in state with his bishops and nobles. In this picture, taken from a contemporary manuscript, the Emperor wears a closed imperial crown and holds a sceptre surmounted by a cross. His footstool is embroidered with representations of the imperial two-headed eagle.

was reburied at El Escorial on 20 January 1980, although a somewhat ludicrous element was provided by the undertaker's assistant who approached the royal catafalque with the crown in one hand and a stepladder in the other in full sight of the congregation.

In Spain's neighbouring country of Portugal the last coronation to take place was that of King John IV, the first of the house of Bragança, at Lisbon on 15 December 1640. The King gave his crown to adorn the statue of Our Lady of Vila Viçosa and thereafter Portuguese sovereigns were not crowned but merely acclaimed. During the Napoleonic Wars the Portuguese royal family and government took refuge in Brazil and the United Kingdom of Portugal, Brazil and the Algarves was proclaimed on 16 December 1815. The following year the Prince Regent succeeded his mad mother Queen Maria I and it was decided to make a momentous occasion of his acclamation, which took place at Rio de Janeiro on 6 February 1818. Accordingly a new crown and sceptre fashioned from Brazilian gold were commissioned and the King took them with him when he returned to Portugal in 1821. The regalia made their appearance at the acclamations of subsequent Portuguese monarchs until that of the last king, Manuel II, in 1908. They are now displayed in the Ajuda Palace in Lisbon and are hardly objects of great beauty.

The Byzantine Emperor Manuel II Paleologus (1391–1425) with the Empress Irene and three of their sons, from a contemporary manuscript. Note that all the family are imperially robed and crowned and carry sceptres in their right hands.

After King John VI had returned to Portugal, Brazil was proclaimed an independent empire under his son, Dom Pedro I, who had remained behind as Regent. He was crowned at Rio on 1 December 1822 with a crown of Brazilian gold, studded with Brazilian diamonds, which was also used for the coronation of his son Dom Pedro II on 18 July 1841. The crown is now displayed in the Palace of Petrópolis. It, too, is of ugly design and shape.

The long tradition of coronation in France had ensured the buildup of a set of regalia comparable to that of England, but during the Revolution it was broken up and sold, as the English regalia had been in 1649. When Napoleon was proclaimed Emperor of the French in 1804, he determined on a consecration and crowning of great magnificence and new regalia were ordered. An item adopted from the old royal regalia was the *Main de Justice* (Hand of Justice), a sceptre surmounted by a carved ivory hand in the act of blessing and symbolic of the monarch's judicial power. Napoleon's Hand of Justice was embellished with jewels from the Carolingian period and is today preserved in the Louvre with other items of his regalia. Napoleon's coronation is well known from David's famous portrayal of the scene, in which Napoleon, anointed by Pope Pius VII and having placed a crown of gold laurel leaves on his own head, is in the act of crowning Josephine, who kneels at his feet. The picture is inaccurate, because Napoleon insisted that his indomitable mother, *Madame Mère*, should be included although, in actual fact, she was not present at the ceremony, of which she disapproved.

When the Bourbons were restored to the French throne in 1814, Louis XVIII declined to have a coronation, which his immense weight and gout would have rendered a distressing ordeal for him. His brother and successor, Charles X, was a far fitter man altogether and his coronation at Rheims on 29 May 1825 was the last ever held in France. Several items of regalia, including the *Sainte Ampoule* with the anointing oil and the sword of Charlemagne, known as 'Joyeuse', had escaped the Revolutionary destruction and were used in the ceremony. Other items were remade for the occasion, including a spendidly jewelled sword which was later stolen from the Louvre and never recovered. Many of the French crown jewels were sold by order of the Third Republic in 1883; those that remain are exhibited in the Galerie d'Apollon in the Louvre.

When the Kingdom of the Netherlands came into being in 1815, King William I commissioned a very substandard set of symbolic regalia, consisting of crown, orb, sceptre and sword made of silver gilt set with imitation gems, which would disgrace a third-rate repertory theatre company. When he abdicated in 1840, he took his crown with him so that his son and successor King William II was obliged to have a new crown made for his inauguration. These very unworthy items of regalia still make their appearance at the inaugurations of Dutch sovereigns, the last time being at the inauguration of Queen Beatrix at Amsterdam on 30 April 1980. The tawdriness of the Dutch crown jewels is rendered all the more ironic by the fact that the personal jewellery owned by the Queen is possibly the most magnificent in Europe, most of it having formed part of the dowry of Queen Anna Pavlovna, the wife of Holland's King William II and daughter of Emperor Paul I of Russia, all of whose daughters were provided with a truly fabulous trousseau.

When Belgium gained its independence from the Kingdom of the Netherlands in 1831 and Queen Victoria's uncle Leopold was elected its first king, the idea of ordering regalia, symbolic or otherwise, appeared ridiculous to the worthy, practical Belgians. Consequently, although there is an Order of the Crown of Belgium and the royal arms are surmounted by an heraldic crown of conventional design, there is no actual crown.

Many items of the regalia of the Holy Roman Emperors survive and the most important will be found mentioned in Appendix 4. Others include the crown of Empress Kunigunde, consort of Emperor Henry II (1002–1024), a gold circlet encrusted with sapphires, rubies, amethysts and pearls, now in the Treasury of the Residenz in Munich; the Byzantine-style crown of Empress Constance of Aragon, consort of Emperor Frederick II, now preserved in Palermo Cathedral; and the

The Holy Roman Emperor Henry IV (1056–1106) as depicted in an illuminated manuscript, enthroned and crowned with a simple open crown. He holds a sceptre surmounted by a dove and the imperial globe, or orb.

crown of Queen Theodolinda of Lombardy, which is kept with the famous Iron Crown (see Appendix 4 under 'Italy') in the Treasury of the Cathedral at Monza.

Of the regalia amassed by the Italian states, those of the Grand Duchy of Tuscany are exhibited in the Pitti Palace at Florence, while those of the Kingdom of the Two Sicilies were pawned by King Francesco II to raise funds for the struggle against Garibaldi, but never redeemed and later broken up and dispersed, and those of the kings of Sardinia were pawned to the Dutch Republic in the eighteenth century and later appropriated and disposed of by the French Revolutionary army.

By far the most beautiful European regalia still existing are those of the Scandinavian kingdoms, of which Sweden's are particularly fine. The Swedish coronation order, used from the time of King Eric XIV (1560–1568), was closely modelled on that of England. Eric's coronation was described by his chaplain, Laurentius Petri Gothus, and commenced with a procession on foot to Uppsala Cathedral, the regalia being carried before the King by the great officers of state and headed by the Key of State, an item unique to Sweden and devised by Eric himself. After the King and other members of the procession had taken their places a sermon was preached. The King then retired behind a silken screen to don the coronation vestments and emerged carrying a vessel full of coins

H. M. KONUNGEN ÖPPNAR URTIMA RIKSDAGEN 1905

which he placed on the altar as an oblation. After further prayers, Eric was stripped to the waist and anointed on the forehead, breast, shoulders, arms and hands. He then received the rest of the coronation vestments and the ring, was girded with the sword, and had the royal mantle placed on his shoulders. After this he took his seat on the throne and was crowned and blessed by the Archbishop, being at once acclaimed by the whole congregation. The investiture with sceptre, orb and Sword of State (not to be confused with the smaller sword with which he had been girt earlier) followed and the herald announced, 'Our most noble and mighty Prince and Lord, Eric XIV, is hereby anointed and proclaimed King of Sweden,' to which those present responded, 'God send our King joy and salvation and grant him long and happily to reign.' The homage of the Princes of the Blood followed and the King created a number of new counts, barons, and knights. The procession then left the Cathedral while the Master of Receipts threw largesse coins among the people. This order, with a few modifications, was followed at all subsequent Swedish coronations until that of Oscar II at Stockholm in 1873, after which the ceremony was abolished.

The ancient regalia of the Russian great princes and tsars are exhibited in the Kremlin Armoury at Moscow together with the later crowns and other items made for Peter the Great after he had been proclaimed Emperor of Russia in 1721. These were used for the first time when Peter

Opposite: King Oscar II of Sweden opening the Riksdag (Parliament) in 1905. This was the last occasion on which the king and princes appeared wearing their robes and crowns. King Oscar's successor, Gustav V, was never crowned and from his accession in 1907 onwards the royal mantle was thrown over the throne and the crown displayed on a table by its side.

The Church of the Assumption in the Kremlin at Moscow was the coronation church of Russian tsars and emperors and the scene of the coronation of Emperor Alexander II, so vividly described (see pages 104 and 113).

This medal struck to commemorate the birth of Peter the Great of Russia in 1672 shows on the obverse his parents Tsar Alexis and Tsaritsa Natalia. The Tsar wears the Russian adaptation of Byzantine imperial robes and the so-called Crown of Vladimir Monomakh and carries a sceptre surmounted by a double-headed eagle and an orb of conventional design.

crowned his wife Catherine at Moscow in May 1724. A very interesting account of the coronation of Emperor Alexander II of Russia on 7 September 1856 was given by Lieutenant-Colonel George Ashley Maude RA, Military Attaché with the Mission headed by Lord Granville which was sent to that event. He wrote to his wife as follows:

> . . . First of all, the Archbishop or Patriarch came upon the Dais and presented the Emperor with a book out of which he read in a clear tone of voice, but in a language which, of course, we did not understand, his Profession of Faith. The Archbishop then read something, which was followed by a beautiful chant, and then the Emperor read something else in a loud and clear tone, and returned the book to the Archbishop. Then more chanting; and I must here remark that although unaccompanied by any music, which is forbidden in the Greek Church, the singing was beautiful throughout. The Emperor then advanced a few steps and knelt down on a cushion. The Archbishop, first making the sign of the Cross three times across the top of his skull, proceeded to bless him, and the responses were chanted in reply. The Emperor then rose, stepped back to the throne, the Grand Duke Constantine removed the collar of the Order of St Andrew, which he wore from his neck, and then proceeded to clothe him with the mantle, which together with that of the Empress, the two crowns, and the globe and sceptre, were all on separate cushions on the table to the left. As soon as he had put on the mantle, he asked for the crown, which was presented to him by the Archbishop and he then *placed it on his own head*. The sceptre and globe were then separately presented to him, he standing all the time. The Empress then moved out to the centre of the Dais, knelt down and was crossed and blest by the Archbishops. She then turned round and knelt in front of her husband, who took off his crown, put it on her head then replaced it on his own. He then asked for her crown, which was quite a small thing, not bigger than my two fists, and placed it on her head, her maids of honour, or ladies in waiting, came forward then to fasten it on, in which they were not very successful, for it fell off two or three times during the course of the ceremony. The Emperor then raised and kissed her on the forehead, not a mere formal kiss but a long loving one, and both their eyes filled with tears; it was very touching. She was then clothed with the Mantle and retired to her throne, and they both for the first time sat down. Then thundered away the guns of the Kremlin, the bells set forth a merry peal and the Choir sang a beautiful chorus. As soon as it was over and the guns had ceased (they fired 101) the old Empress walked across to her son and gave

The Crown of King Eric XIV of Sweden. The crown was made in Stockholm in 1561 by the Flemish goldsmith Cornelius ver Weiden. The rim and arches are goldplated and the cartouches cast in gold and set with unpolished opaque and translucent enamel in a variety of colours as well as pearls, emeralds, rubies and diamonds. The crown is said to have been dropped by the Chancellor Nils Gyllenstierna at the wedding banquet of Eric's Queen Karin Månsdotter in 1568 and to have fallen from the head of King Carl XII when he mounted his horse after his coronation in 1697. Several repairs and alterations have been carried out from time to time. This was the first closed crown to be used in Sweden and was probably closely modelled on the English one.

Queen Maria Eleonora's Crown. This item from the Swedish regalia was made in Stockholm in 1620 by the German goldsmith Rupprecht Miller. It is of gold, partly chased, decorated with black and blue enamel and set with diamonds and rubies. First used for the coronation of Gustav II Adolph's Queen, Maria Eleonora of Brandenburg, the crown was adapted for the coronation of her daughter Queen Christina in 1650, when the four lower arches were added. The crown was widened and further embellished for the coronation of Ulrika Eleonora in 1719 and was also used as the coronation crown of King Adolf Fredrik in 1751.

Queen Lovisa Ulrika's Crown. This very pretty crown was made in Stockholm in 1751 by Andreas Almgren from a design by Jean Eric Rehn, who modelled it on the crown made by the French court jeweller Rondé for the wedding of Marie Leszczynska to Louis XV in 1725. It is of silver, gilt inside, and set with diamonds, the gold orb on top being covered with translucent polished enamel. The crown was made for King Adolf Fredrik's consort Lovisa Ulrika, a sister of Frederick the Great of Prussia, and subsequently used as the coronation crown of Swedish queens.

The Swedish anointing horn of gold, chased and enamelled and set with diamonds and rubies, stands 6 inches (15.5cm) high and was made in Stockholm in 1606 by Peter Kiämpe.

Opposite, below left: King Eric XIV's orb, made in Stockholm in 1561 by Cornelius ver Weiden, who also made Eric's crown, and further embellished in Antwerp by Frantz Beijer in 1568.

Opposite, below right: King Eric XIV's Sceptre. This was made in Stockholm by Hans Heidenrik in 1561 and used at Eric's coronation, although it was not completed until his wedding to Karin Månsdotter in 1568, when extra jewels were added. Later alterations were made in 1719 and 1780.

The Swedish Heir Apparent's Crown. This strange crown was made in 1650 for the then heir apparent Carl Gustav (later King Carl X Gustav) to wear at the coronation of his cousin Queen Christina, where he wore it over a violet-brown coloured hat embroidered in gold and turned up with ermine. The hat was later replaced by a crown cap of blue with gold embroidery and was used by subsequent heirs apparent until 1905, when it was last worn by the future King Gustav V.

Swedish princely crowns. These three crowns were made in Stockholm in 1771 by the court jeweller Johan Adam Marcklin for the two brothers and sister of King Gustav III to wear at his coronation, which took place at Stockholm on 28 May 1772. The princes can be seen wearing their crowns in a contemporary drawing of the coronation. Caps were added in the nineteenth century. Similar crowns were made for other members of the royal family in 1778, 1844, 1860 and 1902.

Above left: The Norwegian King's Crown, made for the Norwegian coronation of King Carl XIV Johan of Sweden and Norway (formerly Napoleon's Marshal Bernadotte) in Trondheim Cathedral on 7 September 1818.

Above right: The Norwegian Queen's Crown, made for the coronation of Queen Désirée, Carl XIV Johan's consort, in 1830, and used to crown subsequent queens of Norway until Queen Maud in 1906.

Right: The Norwegian King's and Queen's Crowns, the Crown of the Heir Apparent, orbs, sceptres, sword and Anointing Horn.

Above: The Crown of King August III of Poland, made for his coronation in 1734. The King was also Elector Friedrich August II of Saxony and used jewels from the Saxon treasury to adorn his crown.

Above right: The Crown of Queen Maria Józefa of Poland, the consort of King August III. It seems strange that the crowns of such a strongly Catholic country as Poland should not be surmounted by the symbol of the cross as in almost all other Christian countries.

The Danish Ampulla. This box to hold the anointing oil was made for the coronation of King Frederik III in 1648 and continued in use until the last Danish coronation in 1840. It is beautifully enamelled and bejewelled, but resembles a biscuit box more than a sacred object.

Above: King Christian IV's Crown. This crown of gold, enamel, pearls and other precious stones was made for King Christian IV of Denmark (1588–1648). It is probably the last crown of open medieval type to be worn by a European monarch.

Left: King Christian V's Crown. The crown made for King Christian V of Denmark in 1671 was used as the coronation crown of his successors until 1840. It is still used at the lying in state of Danish sovereigns.

The Crown of St Stephen. This symbol of the Hungarian monarchy is said to be the crown which
Pope Sylvester III sent to St Stephen when he granted him the title of Apostolic King, although it is of
Byzantine workmanship. It has had an extrememly eventful history (see page 151).

him a long and earnest embrace; there was deep feelings on both sides. The poor old woman trembled with emotion and the young man's face grew pale and his eyes filled . . . The old Lady got through it very well, and after embracing the Empress retired to her own throne. Then came all the brothers, commencing with the Grand Duke Constantine, and they were very hearty and brotherly in their embraces. He held them all in his arms for several seconds and clasped them to his bosom. After them came the Grand Duchesses, and then all his own children. The whole of this scene, which took up a quarter of an hour, was, as you may imagine, of the most interesting description. Several of the Chief Officers of State and Household then came and kissed him on the cheek, most of them he raised to his cheek, others he did not.

After this came the ceremony of Anointing. Both Emperor and Empress went down to the foot of the stairs in front of the altars. They were there received by the Archbishops, the Choir singing all the time, and after some sprinkling with holy water, a gold vessel was produced containing an ointment, called the holy cream. With this they anointed his forehead, eyelids, nose, mouth, ears and finger nails, and it was then wiped off by another with tow, which was afterwards consumed. The Empress was then anointed, but only on the brow . . . The Emperor and Empress then began to descend the stairs and passed out of the North door, and as soon as he was gone, we went out of the South door. We found ourselves in an immense courtyard of the Kremlin, around which were 6 of their ancient churches, including the one we had been in. Every available space had been fitted up in the form of an amphitheatre and all hung with red cloth, the whole filled with ladies and gentlemen. It was a beautiful day and the coup d'oeil was magnificent at a short distance across the courtyard, which was divided into lanes by files of the handsome Chevalier Guard. We saw the Emperor proceeding under a canopy which looked like the roof of a carriage supported on poles. The canopy was carried by 16 General Officers, while 16 Lt. Generals held strings like pall bearers on each side. The Emperor passed through all the churches in succession round the courtyard, and then passed into the Kremlin. Guns firing, bells ringing and bands playing and people shouting making a most tremendous din.

The diplomats were entertained to a 'sumptuous luncheon' in one of the halls of the Kremlin and then taken to the banqueting room to witness the Emperor and the two Empresses being served dinner. The long day ended with illuminations which Maude thought 'they certainly manage to do much better in this country than we do. Every dome and every

Queen Liliuokalani, the last sovereign of the
Hawaiian Islands, who left a graphic account
of the coronation of her brother and predecessor King Kalakaua (see pages 115-17).

minaret was lighted up in the most beautiful manner and instead of
putting a great patch of light, like we do, on one part of the house, they
light up all the architecture, every door and window and pillar and col-
umn showing its outline in glittering lights. They have no gas, but glass
pots full of tallow with a wick in them'.

Although today the United Kingdom is the only country among
Europe's surviving monarchies to have retained the coronation ceremony,
coronations still take place in several Asian countries and, although non-
Christian, the consecration, dedication and setting apart of the monarch
are basic to all of them. The kings of Thailand are crowned in a Buddhist
ceremony, as also the kings of Bhutan; the kings of Nepal receive their
crowns surrounded by Hindu ritual and symbolism; and the sultans of
Malaysia are crowned and blessed with simple Muslim rites.

Only one other country apart from Britain crowns its monarchs with
Christian rites, the Kingdom of Tonga in the Pacific. The Tongan
sovereigns, moreover, are the only ones who belong to the Methodist

King Kalakaua's Crown, made in England for
his coronation as King of Hawaii in 1883. The
gems with which it is set replace the originals,
which were prised out and sold after the
crown jewels were looted by a soldier in 1898.

Church, which is the state religion, and they are crowned with simple yet
impressive ceremonial in the Royal Chapel at Nuku'alofa, the capital. Yet
the kings and queens of Tonga are not the only Polynesian monarchs to
have been crowned, as Hawaii, now the Fiftieth State of the United States
of America, was the scene of one impressive coronation.

The Hawaiian islands had been united into one kingdom under King
Kamehameha I (*d*1819), whose descendants embraced Christianity and
reigned until December 1872, when King Kamehameha V died childless
without nominating an heir. The constitution provided for this contin-
gency by means of an election and the vacant throne was filled on this
occasion by a close kinsman of the late King, who reigned as Lunalilo I.
Unfortunately, he was of a delicate constitution and died after a reign of
one year, also childless and without nominating a successor, so that
another election was called for. The candidates were Queen Emma, the
widow of King Kamehameha IV, the brother and predecessor of
Kamehameha V, and Colonel David Kalakaua, the descendant of several

great lines of chiefs. Kalakaua proved successful and was duly elected King on 12 February 1874. Although married, he was childless, so he at once promoted his surviving brother and two sisters to royal rank and the brother was proclaimed heir presumptive. When he died on 10 April 1877, the elder sister Princess Liliuokalani was proclaimed heiress presumptive and it is to her that we are indebted for a delightful account of her brother's coronation. After nine years on the throne King Kalakaua decided, as his sister wrote, 'to formally ratify the accession of the new dynasty to the Hawaiian throne by investing both His Majesty Kalakaua, and his queen, Kapiolani, with the crown and other insignia of royalty'. Princess Liliuokalani's record of the proceedings continues:

> The two crowns were made in England, and were of gold studded with precious stones; from the same country came also the dresses of the queen and those of her sisters, the Princess Poomaikalani and the Princess Kekaulike. My toilets were furnished from Paris dressmaking establishments, and consisted of two complete costumes. The gown to be worn during the day at the coronation ceremony was of gold and white brocaded silk; that intended for the *soirée* and the royal ball was of crimson satin; each costume was perfect in itself, the lesser details being in harmony with the dress; both were heavily embroidered, and were generally considered to have been the most elegant productions of Parisian art ever seen in Hawaii on this or any other state occasion. My sister, the Princess Likelike, had sent to San Francisco for her wardrobe, which, like mine, consisted of two complete costumes, one of which was of white silk of figured brocade handsomely trimmed with pearls; her full evening dress was of silk, in color or shade styled at that time 'moonlight-on-the-lake,' and, with head-dress to match, it was very effective . . .
> Promptly at the appointed time His Majesty Kalakaua, King of the Hawaiian Islands, accompanied by Her Majesty Kapiolani, his queen, made their appearance. I give the order of the procession to the royal pavilion. Princess Kekaulike, bearing the royal feather cloak, and with her the Princess Poomaikalani; then the Princess Likelike, with the child-princess Kaiulani, and her father, Hon A.S. Cleghorn; Governor Dominis [Liliuokalani's husband], and myself; we were all attended by our *kahili* bearers, and those ancient staffs of royalty were held aloft at our sides. Then followed Prince Kawananakoa, bearing one of the crowns, and Prince Kalanianaole bearing the other crown, succeeded by two others of noble birth and lineage bearing insignia of royalty of either native or traditional usage, the *tabu* sticks, the sceptre, and ring. Then came Their Majesties the King and Queen, attended by their *kahili* bearers, who

stationed themselves just inside the pavilion. As the royal party entered, the queen was immediately attended by her ladies in waiting, eight in number, all attired in black velvet trimmed with white satin. The long and handsome train of Her Majesty's robe was carried by two ladies of high rank and of noble lineage, Keano and Kekaulike.

The ceremonies were opened with prayer by Rev. Mr.Mackintosh; and then followed one of those coincidences which are so striking on any such occasion, and was certainly noticed as one of the most beautiful incidents of the day. In the very act of prayer, just as he put forth his hand to lift the crown, before placing it on the brow of the king, a mist, or cloud, such as may gather very quickly in our tropical climate, was seen to pass over the sun, obscuring its light for a few minutes; then at the moment when the king was crowned there appeared, shining so brilliantly as to attract general attention, a single star. It was noticed by the entire multitude assembled to witness the pageant, and a murmur of wonder and admiration passed over the throng. The ceremonies proceeded with due solemnity, and the whole scene was very impressive and not to be forgotten. At its close the company retired to the palace in the same order as that in which it had come forth; and the day ceremonies being over the crowd dispersed, retiring to rest from the fatigues and excitements of the day, so as to be able to enter with zest into the festivities of the evening, as a grand ball was to be given at the palace. Indeed, the entire grounds were given up to pleasure such as can only be fully imagined by those who have actually mingled with a happy people in the festivities of a tropical night.

Eight years after the event she described so vividly, Liliuokalani succeeded her brother on the Hawaiian throne, but her reign was destined to be a short and troubled one, ending in her deposition in 1893. The Queen lived on as a private citizen until her death in 1917, when she was granted a state funeral by the American government. The occasion was marked by one of those incidents in which Liliuokalani herself would doubtless have seen the hand of providence. As her coffin was carried into the Royal Mausoleum, the bearers misjudged the height of the doorway so that the crown which had graced the brow of Kalakaua was swept from its top and fell to the ground.

Today many of the splendid artefacts which were commissioned throughout the world to exalt and glorify the rulers of nations remain to testify to lost splendours, but some at least still fulfil their original purpose and hopefully may long continue so to do.

APPENDIX 1

Glossary of Heraldic Terms

Words in *italics* will be found listed (in their simplest form) elsewhere in the Glossary.

ABASED Description applied to a *charge* when placed below its usual position.

ABATEMENT A mark of degradation.

ACCOSTED Side by side.

ACCOUCHÉ Descriptive of a shield suspended from one corner by a ribbon or belt.

ACCRUED Descriptive of trees in full growth.

ACHIEVEMENT A full coat of arms with *crest, helmet, mantling, shield, motto,* and (where applicable) *coronet* of rank, *supporters* and insignia of orders.

ADDORSED Back to back.

AFFRONTY (in older *blazons* AFFRONTÉE) Full face.

À LA CUISSE 'At the thigh'. Descriptive of a disembodied leg.

ALLERION A beakless and legless eagle.

ALLUMY (in older blazons ALLUMÉE) Descriptive of the eyes of animals when the pupils are flecked with red.

AMBULANT Walking.

ANCHOR Always depicted without rope or chain attached unless *blazoned* 'cabled'. The barbs are called flukes and the crossbar, if of a different *tincture* from the rest of the anchor, is described as 'beamed' of that colour.

ANCHORED (also ANCRED) Applied to a cross of which the four arms are barbed like the fluke of an anchor.

ANCIENT A small flag or pennon on the stern of a ship.

ANNULET A ring; the *cadency* mark used to distinguish the arms of a fifth son.

ANTELOPE This can be depicted as either an heraldic antelope or the natural animal. The heraldic antelope (based on an inadequate knowledge of natural history in medieval times) has a stag's body and legs, cloven hooves, a tusk growing out of its snout, serrated horns, and a *lion's* tail.

ANTIQUE CROWN (also known as an EASTERN CROWN) A crown composed of five or more sharp points mounted on a circlet.

APPAUMY (in older *blazons* APPAUMÉE) Descriptive of an open hand with the palm facing.

ARBALESTE A crossbow.

ARCHED Descriptive of a *charge* when curved.

ARGENT Silver or white; abbreviated to arg.

ARMED Descriptive of an animal with horns, teeth, tusks and talons of a different *tincture* from the body. Swans, geese, and birds without talons, however, are described as 'beaked and membered'.

ARMIGER A person entitled to bear arms is an armiger and may be described as being armigerous.

ARQUEBUS An antique gun.

ASSURGEANT Descriptive of anything arising from water.

ASTRAL CROWN A crown composed of four stars (three being visible) set between pairs of elevated wings mounted on a circlet.

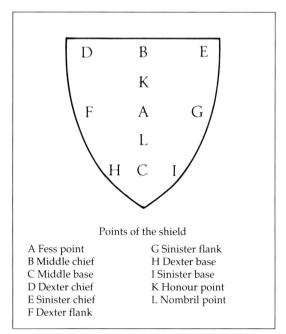

Points of the shield

A Fess point   G Sinister flank
B Middle chief   H Dexter base
C Middle base   I Sinister base
D Dexter chief   K Honour point
E Sinister chief   L Nombril point
F Dexter flank

ATTIRED Descriptive of deer and similar animals when bearing horns.

AUGMENTATION A special mark of honour or favour granted by the sovereign as an addition to the family arms, often to commemorate some worthy deed. An example is the *inescutcheon* granted to the 14th Earl of Strathmore and Kinghorne (to be borne by successive *earls*) in commemoration of his daughter Elizabeth (now HM Queen Elizabeth The Queen Mother) becoming Queen Consort.

AZURE Blue; abbreviated to az.

BADGE Badges do not form an integral part of armorial bearings, but may be shown placed below the *motto*, or, if more than one, on each side of the *crest*.

BANDED Anything encircled by a cord or rope is so described, eg a sheaf of corn.

BANNER The heraldic banner is a square-shaped flag bearing a representation of the owner's arms as they appear on his *shield*.

BAR A band or bar, one-fifth the total depth of a *shield* running horizontally across its width.

BAR SINISTER A popular misnomer employed by novelists and journalists, who believe it to be a heraldic sign denoting bastardy. No such *charge* exists, although *bend sinisters* and *baton sinisters* have occasionally been used in the arms granted to royal bastards.

BARBED A term used in reference to (a) the human beard (b) the leaves of a full-blown heraldic *rose* (c) the points of an arrow, fish-hook, or spear (d) ears of wheat (e) a fully *caparisoned* horse.

BARON The fifth and lowest rank of the peerage. A baron's *coronet* consists of a plain gilt circlet surmounted by six silver balls, four of which are shown when it is depicted heraldically.

BARON AND FEMME, PER Descriptive of the *impaled* arms of a husband and wife.

BARONESS The wife of a *baron*, or a peeress in her own right.

BARONET The lowest hereditary title, instituted by King James I in 1611. Baronets have the prefix of 'Sir' and their wives that of 'Lady'. The insignia consist of a neck badge.

BARS GEMEL Two *bars* or *barrulets* placed parallel to each other.

BARRULET A diminutive of the *bar*.

BARRY Descriptive of a shield divided into horizontal *bars* of alternate *tinctures* and an even number of divisions, eg barry of six, *argent* and *sable* would indicate six alternating divisions of silver and black.

BASE The bottom portion of a *shield*.

BASILISK An heraldic monster similar to a *wyvern* or *cockatrice*, but having a *dragon's* head at the end of its tail.

BASINET A type of steel *helmet*.

BATON A short staff, always depicted in *bend* and *couped*. Often used in the arms of royal bastards, particularly those granted to the sons of King Charles II.

BATTERING RAM An instrument anciently used to batter down the doors and walls of besieged cities and castles; it is depicted heraldically with the operative end facing *dexter*.

BATTLED Descriptive of a *charge* when it is drawn to represent the battlements of a castle. See also *embattled*.

BATTLED ARRONDIE Descriptive of a battlement rounded at the top.

BATTLED-IMBATTLED A double battlement.

BAY, AT Descriptive of a stag with head lowered in defence.

BEACON Usually depicted as an iron fire basket on top of a high pole, against which a ladder is placed.

BEAKED *Armed*; used for swans, geese and birds without talons.

BEARING A term applicable to any single *charge* or heraldic device.

BEND A band, formed of two parallel straight lines, extending from the *dexter chief* of a *shield* to the *sinister base* and normally one-third in width of the total length of the *shield*. If it runs the reverse way it is always called a 'bend *sinister*'.

BENDLET A diminutive of the *bend*, half its width. It is never shown with any *device* upon it.

BENDY Descriptive of a *field* divided diagonally into four, six, eight, or more equal parts.

BEZANT (or TALENT) A Byzantine gold coin, always represent as a round gold disc.

BEZANTY Strewn with *bezants*.

BILLET A rectangle depicted with the shorter side downwards.

BILLETY Strewn with *billets*.

BIRD-BOLT A small arrow with a blunt head.

BLACKAMOOR Descriptive of any black man.

BLAZON The heraldic description of a coat of arms couched in heraldic language.

BORDURE A band or border running round the edge of a *shield* and giving the appearance of a frame. A bordure *wavy* is sometimes used to denote bastardy.

BOTONNY (in older blazons BOTONÉE) Descriptive of a *cross* in which the arms terminate in *trefoils*.

BOUGET See *water bouget*.

BOURDONNÉ Descriptive of a cross in which the arms terminate in ovals set at right angles.

BOWED *Embowed*, or *arched*.

BRASSARTS Armour for the elbows and arms.

BROAD ARROW An arrowhead, differenced from the *pheon* by having the inside of the prongs smooth.

BURGONET A steel *helmet* worn by foot soldiers.

CABOSSED or CABOSHED Descriptive of an animal's head shown full face without any neck visible.

CADENCY The system whereby a coat of arms is differenced to indicate the position of an individual bearer within the family; in England now rarely used outside the royal family. The eldest son would *charge* his paternal arms with a *label*; the second with a *crescent*; the third with a *mullet*; the fourth with a *martlet*; the fifth with an *annulet*; the sixth with a *fleur-de-lis*. A second son of a third son would use a *mullet* charged with a *crescent* and so on. A different system obtains in Scotland, employing *bordures*.

CADUCEUS A winged wand, or staff, with two snakes entwined around it. In Greek and Roman mythology it was the rod carried by Hermes (Mercury).

CALTRAP (or GALTRAP) An iron instrument of four points, so arranged that when flung on the ground one point was always upwards, used in medieval times to wound horses' feet and thus impede the advance of cavalry.

CALVARY CROSS (also called PASSION CROSS) A cross mounted on three steps.

CAMELOPARD The heraldic name for a giraffe, which medieval naturalists believed to be a cross between a camel and a leopard.

CANTING ARMS Arms which allude in a punning way to the name or profession of the holder, eg swans as *charges* for a person named Swann, or a book or quill pen to denote a writer.

CANTING MOTTOES Similar to *canting arms*, these may incorporate a pun on the name of the holder, eg the motto of the Vernons is 'Vernon *Semper Viret*' (Vernon always flourishes), which may also be rendered as 'Ver Non Semper Viret' (spring does not always flourish).

CANTON A divison of the *shield* consisting of a rectangle placed in the *dexter* top corner occupying approximately one-third of the *chief*.

CAP-A-PIE Head to toe. A man in full armour is described as armed cap-a-pie.

CAP OF MAINTENANCE A cap of state of crimson (occasionally blue) velvet, turned up with ermine. An actual cap of maintenance is worn by male sovereigns in the opening stages of the coronation ceremony and is borne on a staff before the sovereign at the State Opening of Parliament. The heraldic cap of maintenance is the insignia of Scottish feudal barons and French seigneurs.

CAPARISON The trappings of a warhorse.

CARTOUCHE An oval sometimes used as an alternative to the *lozenge* to display the arms of ladies. It is also sometimes used for the arms of Popes and church dignitaries, the ordinary *shield* being deemed inappropriate to their calling.

CASQUE A *helmet*.

CASTLE A frequent *charge*, usually depicted as two battlemented towers connected by a short battlemented wall with a portcullised doorway in the centre.

CAT-A-MOUNTAIN A wild cat, resembling an ordinary cat but with tufted ears.

CATHERINE WHEEL A six-spoked wheel with the spokes projecting through the rim and ending in short curved blades, representing the instrument of martyrdom of St Catherine.

CELESTIAL CROWN An *antique* or *Eastern crown* in which the points teminate in a star.

CENTAUR (also SAGITTARIUS) A mythical creature with the head, arms and trunk of a man springing from a horse's body, usually depicted holding a bow and arrow.

CHAPEAU See *cap of maintenance*.

CHAPLET A *garland* or *wreath* of flowers or leaves.

CHARGE Any device or figure placed upon a *shield*.

CHARGED Descriptive of anything bearing *charges*.

CHARGER A large dish or plate.

CHEQUY (or CHECKY) A *field* divided into small squares of alternate *tinctures*.

CHERUB Usually represented as a child's head between two wings.

CHESS ROOK The heraldic version of this game piece is quite different from the rook or castle actually used in the game of chess. The heraldic name is *zule*.

CHEVRON A division of the *shield* resembling a reversed V and usually one-third of the depth of the *shield*. It always reaches to the sides of the *shield* and its edges may be plain, *engrailed, invested, embattled* etc.

CHEVRONEL A diminutive of the *chevron*, one-third to one-half its width, usually depicted in pairs.

CHIEF The top portion of a *shield*, marked by a line drawn parallel to the top of the *shield* and about one-third down.

CHIMERA An heraldic monster with a maiden's face, a *lion's* mane and legs, a goat's body, and a *dragon's* tail.

CINQUEFOIL A five-lobed leaf.

CIVIC CROWN A *garland* of oakleaves and acorns set on a rim.

CLARION A lance rest.

CLOSET A diminutive of the *bar*, slightly larger than a *barrulet*.

COCKATRICE An heraldic monster with the head, beak, comb, wattles and legs of a cock, and the wings, tail and body of a *wyvern*.

COMBATANT Descriptive of two *charges rampant* face to face.

COMPONY (GOBONY) Descriptive of a border, *pale, bend*, or other *ordinary*, made up by alternating squares of metals and colours. Two such rows are described as compony counter-compony.

CONJOINED Joined together.

CONJOINED IN LURE A pair of wings joined together at the bases with the tips pointing downwards.

CORNISH CHOUGH A bird resembling a raven with red beak and legs.

CORNUCOPIA A ram's horn with an abundance of fruit cascading from the open end; also known as the 'horn of plenty'.

CORONET The lesser crown worn by members of the royal family and peers and their wives. The design differs according to rank. Coronets are actually worn at coronations in this country as well as being depicted heraldically in armorial bearings. In other countries of Europe they are only used heraldically.

COTISED (sometimes COTTISED) Descriptive of a *charge* depicted with one of its diminutives, eg a *bendlet*, on each side of it.

COUCHANT Descriptive of an animal lying down with head raised.

COUNTER-CHANGED (INTER-CHANGED) A *shield* or *charge* divided into two parts in which the *tinctures* are reversed.

COUNTER-EMBOWED Bent with the elbow to the *sinister*, or bent in a reverse direction.

COUNTER-FLORY A *tressure flory* in which the alternate *fleurs-de-lis* are reversed.

COUNTER-POTENT An heraldic fur, the reverse of *potent*.

COUNTER-VAIR An heraldic fur, the reverse of *vair*.

COUNTESS The wife of an *earl*, or a peeress in her own right. Also the wife of a Continental count.

COUPED Descriptive of a head or limb shown severed from the body, or anything shown as cut off.

COUPLE-CLOSE A diminutive of the *chevron*, always borne in pairs.

COURANT Running.

COWARD Descriptive of an animal with its tail between its legs.

CRAMPET The steel tip at the end of a scabbard.

CRENELLATED See *embattled*.

CRESCENT A half or three-quarter moon depicted with the horns turned upwards.

CRESSET See *beacon*.

CREST Originally the device worn on the *helmet* for identification purposes. Now the device displayed above the *shield* and an integral part of the coat of arms. Unfortunately, in popular parlance the term is very commonly misused to refer to the whole *achievement*.

CREST CORONET A *coronet* used in a *crest* and not denoting rank, formerly referred to as a *ducal coronet* but differing from the actual *coronet* of a *duke*.

CRINED Haired or maned.

CRONEL The iron head of a tilting spear.

CROSIER or PASTORAL STAFF The staff borne by bishops and abbots and shaped like a shepherd's crook.

CROSS One of the commonest heraldic *ordinaries*. There are very many varieties, some of which are listed below.

CROSS-CROSSLET A *cross* in which the arms are also *crosses*.

CROSS MOLINE See illustration.

CROSS PATY (in older *blazons* PATTÉE) See illustration.

CROSS PATY FITCHY See illustration.

CROSS PATY QUADRATE See illustration.

CROSS POTENT See illustration.

CROWN The headdress of gold or precious metal denoting sovereign rank. In English heraldry it is depicted as a stylized version of St Edward's Crown, the actual coronation crown. In Scottish heraldry it is a version of the Crown of Scotland. The reader is referred to the Regalia section of this book and Appendix 2 for more details.

CRUSILLY *Powdered* with *crosses*.

CUBIT ARM A hand and arm severed below the elbow.

CUISSES The armour covering the thigh and the knee.

DANCETTY (in older blazons DANCETTÉE) A triangular *indentation*.

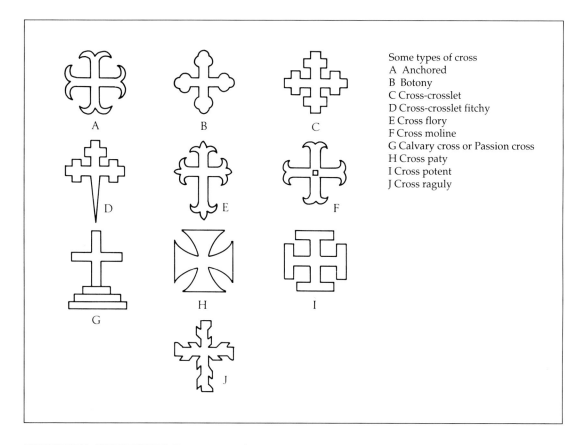

Some types of cross
A Anchored
B Botony
C Cross-crosslet
D Cross-crosslet fitchy
E Cross flory
F Cross moline
G Calvary cross or Passion cross
H Cross paty
I Cross potent
J Cross raguly

DEBRUISED (OPPRESSED) Descriptive of any *charge* over which an *ordinary* or *sub-ordinary* is placed.

DECHAUSSÉ Dismembered limbs of an animal set at a slight distance from the trunk.

DECKED Descriptive of the feathers of a bird when the edges are bordered with a thin line of a different *tincture*.

DECOLLATED Beheaded.

DECRESCENT A *crescent* moon with the horns facing towards the *sinister*.

DEFAMED Without a tail.

DEMI Half.

DETRIMENT, MOON IN HER The moon in eclipse.

DEXTER The right side, which in heraldry is the left side of the arms to the observer.

DIFFERENCE, MARKS OF See *cadency*.

DIMIDIATED Divided into two equal parts; the early method of *impalement* whereby two coats were cut in half by a vertical line running down the centre of the *shield*. No longer used.

DISARMED A creature depicted without beak, claws, teeth, horns, etc.

DISCLOSED A creature with its wings displayed and inverted.

DISMEMBERED See *dechaussé*.

DISPLAYED With wings out (expanded), usually descriptive of birds.

DISPONED Arranged.

DISTILLING Applied to blood or any other liquid falling in drops.

DORMANT Sleeping.

DOUBLE-QUEUED Two tailed.

DOUBLED Descriptive of *mantling* twisted to show the underside.

DOVETAILED A method of partition.

DRAGON An heraldic monster.

DRAPEAU A flag.

DUCHESS The wife of a *duke*, or a peeress in her own right.

DUKE The highest rank in the peerage. A duke's *coronet* consists of a gilt circlet, *chased as jewelled*, surmounted by eight strawberry leaves, five of which are shown when the *coronet* is depicted heraldically. The former description of ducal *coronet* to denote a *coronet* not indicative of rank has now been replaced by *crest coronet*.

EAGLE A very common *charge* in heraldry, represented in many different way and often two headed.

EARL The third rank in the peerage. The title is equivalent to the Continental count and the wife of an earl is called a *countess*. An earl's *coronet* consists of a gilt circlet, *chased as jewelled*, surmounted by eight silver balls on eight tall gold spikes alternating with gold strawberry leaves. When depicted heraldically, five spikes and four strawberry leaves are shown.

EASTERN CROWN See *antique crown*.

ELEVATED Descriptive of the wings of birds when the tips point upwards.

EMBATTLED A line of partition which is indented to resemble the battlements of a tower or castle.

EMBOWED Anything bent or bowed.

EMBRUED (IMBRUED) Dripping with blood.

ENDORSE A diminutive of the *pale*.

ENDORSED See *addorsed*.

ENFIELD An heraldic monster, having the head and tail of a fox, the forefeet of an *eagle* and the hind legs of a wolf. It is the *crest* of the O'Kelly family.

ENFILED A *charge* surrounded by a circlet or *coronet*.

ENGRAILED A *scalloped* line of partition in which the spikes point outwards.

ENHANCED Descriptive of an *ordinary* placed higher than its normal position.

ENSIGNED Descriptive of a *charge* placed above another.

EQUIPPED Descriptive of a fully *caparisoned* horse.

ERADICATED A tree or plant torn up by the roots.

ERASED A head or limb torn from the body.

ERECT Upright.

ERMINE A white fur with black spots.

ERMINES A black fur with white spots.

ERMINOIS A gold fur with black spots.

ESCALLOP A cockle shell.

ESCARBUNCLE A rimless wheel of eight spokes radiating from an embossed centre and terminating in *fleurs-de-lis*. It is said to represent a precious stone (the carbuncle), but seems more likely to represent the strengthening bosses of a shield.

ESCROLL See *scroll*.

ESCUTCHEON A small *shield* borne in the centre of a larger *shield* and used to display the arms of a wife who is an *armigerous* heiress. In Continental heraldry it is used to display the arms of a parent family over arms of dominion.

ESTOILE A star with six *wavy* points.

EVETT A lizard-like animal occurring in the arms of some ancient Irish families.

EXPANDED See *displayed*.

FALCHION A type of sword.

FASCES A bundle of rods tied together with an axe in the centre, often found in the arms of judges and magistrates.

FEATHERED Applied to arrows when the plume is of a different *tincture* from the shaft.

FER-DE-FOURCHETTE Descriptive of all *crosses* and *saltires* with extremities ending in a forked iron.

FER-DE-MOLINE See *millrind*.

FESS (or FESSE) A division of the *shield* consisting of a horizontal band extending across the centre and one-third of the total depth.

FESS POINT The centre of a *shield*.

FIELD The surface of the *shield* upon which all *charges* are depicted.

FILE See *label*.

FILLET A diminutive of the *chief*, usually one-fourth its width.

FIMBRIATED A *charge* bordered with a narrow edge of a different *tincture*.

FITCHY (in older *blazons* FITCHÉE) Pointed at the end.

FLAUNCHES (or FLANCHES) Divisions of the *field* consisting of two curved lines drawn from the extreme top corners of the *shield* to parallel points in the base.

FLEUR-DE-LIS The heraldic lily; used as a *cadency* mark to denote a sixth son.

FLORY (also FLEURY) Flowered with *fleurs-de-lis*.

FLORY COUNTER-FLORY Descriptive of a *charge* edged with *fleurs-de-lis* placed alternately pointing outwards and inwards.

FLOTANT Floating; applied both to a *banner* floating in the air and to a ship.

FOLIATED Leaved.

FORCENE Descriptive of a horse rearing on its hind legs.

FOUNTAIN Represented by a *roundle barry wavy* of six *argent* and *azure*.

FOURCHÉE Forked at the end.

FRACTED Broken.

FRET A *saltire* and *mascle* interlaced.

FRETTY A *field* covered with interlaced parallel *bars* as in a trellis.

FRUCTED Bearing fuit.

FULGENT Rayed.

FUMANT Smoking.

FURNISHED Descriptive of a fully *caparisoned* horse.

FUSIL An elongated *lozenge*.

FUSILLY Covered with *fusils*.

FYLFOT A type of *cross* resembling a swastika.

GADS Plates of steel or iron.

GALLEY See *lymphad*.

GALTRAP See *caltrap*.

GAMB The foreleg or paw of an animal.

GARB A sheaf of grain, always shown as wheat unless otherwise specified.

GARBED Clothed.

GARDEBRAS The elbow piece of a suit of armour.

GARDE-VISURE The *vizor* of a *helmet*.

GARLAND A *wreath* of leaves or flowers.

GARNISHED Decorated; usually applied to armour.

GAUNTLET An iron or steel glove.

GED A pike (in Scottish heraldry).

GEM RING A ring set with precious stones.

GEMEL COLLAR A collar formed of two independent rings.

GENET (a) A small horse of Spanish breed (b) a civet or musk cat (c) the broom plant (*planta genista*).

GENUANT Kneeling.

GILLYFLOWER A red, five-pointed flower, probably representing a carnation.

GIRAFFE See *camelopard*.

GIRDED (also GIRT) Bound about with a band or girdle.

GLAIVE A javelin.

GLISSANT Gliding, as applied to snakes.

GLORY Descriptive of an object surrounded by rays.

GOBONY See *compony*.

GOLPE A purple *roundle*, also known as a wound.

GORGED Collared.

GORGES A whirlpool.

GORGET Neck armour.

GRADIENT Descriptive of a tortoise walking.

GRAPPLING IRON An implement used in naval warfare, depicted as an anchor with four flukes.

GREAVE Leg armour.

GREYHOUND A common heraldic *charge*.

GRICE A young wild boar.

GRIECES Steps, or degrees, on which *crosses* are sometimes placed. See *Calvary*.

GRIFFIN An heraldic monster with the upper half of an *eagle* and the lower half of a *lion*. Ears are always added to the head.

GRIFFIN-MALE The same as a *griffin* but without wings and with spikes or rays.

GUARDANT Full faced.

GUIDON A pennon carried by horsemen.

GULES Red; abbreviated to gu.

GUTTÉ Stewn with drops.

GUTTÉ D'EAU Strewn with drops of water.

GUTTÉ DE LARMES Strewn with tears.

GUTTÉ DE POIX Strewn with pitch or black drops.

GUTTÉ DE SANG Strewn with blood.

GUTTÉ D'HUILE (or GUTTÉ D'OLIVE) Stewn with drops of oil (coloured *vert*).

GUTTÉ D'OR Strewn with drops of gold.

GUTTÉ REVERSED Drops shown inverted.

GUZE A *roundle* of blood colour.

GYRON A triangular divison of the *field* formed by two lines, one in *bend* and one in *fess*, meeting at the centre point.

GYRONNY A *shield* divided into triangular portions from six to twelve in number.

HABERGEON A short, sleeveless coat of mail.

HABITED Clothed.

HARPY An heraldic monster with the head and bust of a woman and the lower parts of a vulture.

HART A stag.

HATCHMENT A corruption of *achievement*. A hatchment was a painting on board of the arms of a deceased person, formerly placed over the main door of the house where the dead person lay and moved to the parish church after the funeral. Many examples survive and are frequently to be seen in country churches.

HAUBERK *Habergeon*.

HAURIANT Descriptive of a fish standing on its tail in a vertical position.

HEAD A common *charge*, both of man and animal.

HELMET The conventions governing the representation of helmets are dealt with in the main text (page 24).

HEMP BREAK An implement used for breaking and bruising hemp or flax.

HILL Depicted as a high grassy mound.

HIND A female stag.

HIPPOCAMPUS A sea horse.

HIPPOGRIFF An heraldic monster having the top part of a *griffin* and the lower part of a horse.

HONOUR POINT The point of a *shield* between middle *chief* point and *fess* point.

HUMETTY (in older *blazons* HUMETTÉE) Descriptive of an *ordinary* which is *couped* so that its extremities do not reach the edges of the *shield*.

HURST A small clump of trees.

HURT A blue *roundel*.

HURTY (in older *blazons* HURTÉE) *Powdered* with *hurts*.

HYDRA A seven-headed monster.

IBEX Not the actual animal, but an imaginary beast resembling an heraldic *antelope* with two straight serrated horns.

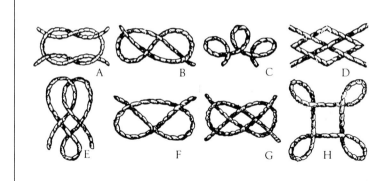

Examples of heraldic knots
A Bourchier knot
B Cavendish knot
C Hungerford knot
D Harington knot, also known as true lovers' knot
E Heneage
F Stafford knot
G Wake (or Ormond) knot
H Bowen's knot

IMBRUED *Embrued*.

IMPALEMENT The arrangement of two coats of arms side by side on one *shield*. A husband's arms may be impaled with those of his wife and a bishop's with those of his see.

INCENSED Descriptive of an animal with flames of fire gushing from its mouth and ears.

INCREMENT (or INCRESCENT) Descriptive of the *crescent* moon when the horns face the *dexter* side of the *shield*.

INDENTED Descriptive of a *serrated* line of more than three points.

INESCUTCHEON A small *shield* borne as a *charge* on a larger *shield*.

INFLAMED Burning.

INFULA A diadem.

IN LURE Two wings *conjoined* with the tips pointing downwards.

IN PRIDE Applied to a peacock or turkey with its tail displayed.

IN SPLENDOUR Applied to the sun surrounded by rays.

INTER-CHANGED See *counter-changed*.

INVECTED The reverse of *engrailed*.

INVERTED AND CONJOINED Turned the wrong way.

ISSUANT Issuing from.

JACENT A treetrunk, or similar *charge*, lying in a horizontal position.

JAVELIN A throwing spear.

JELLOP The comb of a cock, hen, etc.

JERUSALEM CROSS A *cross* with a *couped cross* in each angle.

JESSANT Descriptive of a half-figure arising from a *fess* or other *ordinary*.

JESSANT-DE-LIS Descriptive of a *fleur-de-lis* passing through a *leopard's* face through the mouth and emerging at the back of the head.

JESSES The leather thongs which fasten the bells to the legs of hunting birds.

JEWELLED, CHASED AS Descriptive of the circlet of a peer's *coronet* when it is embossed to represent being set with precious stones.

JUPON A surcoat.

KNOTS Many varieties of knot are found in heraldry (see illustration).

LABEL (or FILE) The distinctive *cadency* mark of the eldest son. It was originally a piece of linen, or other material, with three points, attached to the paternal *shield*. In royal heraldry all the children of the sovereign are assigned labels of three points with different *charges* superimposed to distinguish them. Grandchildren of a sovereign are assigned labels of five points.

LAMBREQUIN See *mantling*.

LANGUED Tongued.

LEOPARD The *lions* of England were at one time blazoned as leopards.

LINED The inside lining of any mantle, cap, etc.

LION A very common *charge*.

LIONCEL A young *lion*; formerly used when more than three *lions* appeared together on a *shield*.

LIVERY COLOURS The colours worn by liveried servants were based on the two chief *tinctures* of the family coat of arms. Colours of red and gold are used by the royal family alone. Other families with these colours must use substitutes, eg maroon and buff.

LOZENGE (a) A diamond-shaped *charge* (b) the *field* on which a lady's arms are displayed.

LOZENGY Descriptive of a *field* covered with *lozenges*.

LUCE The heraldic name for pike.

LYMPHAD A galley, or heraldic ship.

MAIDEN'S HEAD The head and neck of a woman *couped* either at the shoulders or the breast.

MAILED Clothed in mail armour.

MALTESE CROSS A *cross* of eight points

MANTICORA (also MAN-TIGER) A fabulous monster with the head of a man, the horns of an ox, and a *lion's* body.

MANTLING (LAMBREQUIN) The name given to the cloth covering the *helmet* and held in place by the *crest wreath*.

MARCHIONESS The wife of a *marquess*, or a peeress in her own right.

MARQUESS The second rank in the peerage between *duke* and *earl*. A marquess's *coronet* is composed of a gilt circlet, *chased as jewelled*, surmounted by four silver balls and four strawberry leaves alternately. When depicted heraldically, three leaves and two balls are shown. The spelling 'marquis' should never be used for British noblemen.

MARSHALLING The art of correctly arranging armorial bearings.

MARTLET A fabulous bird resembling a swallow without legs, being tufted at the thighs. It is the *cadency* mark of a fourth son.

MASCLE A *lozenge voided*.

MASONED Descriptive of a *charge* drawn to represent masonry.

MAUNCH An old-fashioned sleeve with a long, hanging cuff. It is the *charge* of the Hastings family.

MEMBERED Applied to the beaks, legs etc of birds and animals when *tinctured* differently from the rest of the body.

MERLE A blackbird.

MERMAID A fabulous creature with the top half of a woman and the bottom half of a fish, usually represented with a comb and looking-glass.

MERMAN The male version of a *mermaid*, usually represented with flowing hair and beard and holding a trident.

MILLRIND (FER-DE-MOLINE) The heraldic representation of the iron retaining-piece which is fixed in the centre of a millstone.

MITRE The headdress worn by bishops and abbots. The mitre of the Bishop of Durham is set within a *ducal coronet* to denote the palatine jurisdiction formerly held by that prelate.

MOOR'S HEAD The heraldic description of a black man's head *couped* at the neck.

MORSE A sea lion.

MOTTO See main text (page 28).

MOUND The heraldic name given to the piece of regalia usually known as an orb.

MOUNT Descriptive of the bottom of the *shield* when shown as a curved, grassy field.

MOUNTED Descriptive of a rider on a horse or other animal.

MULLET A star of five points, unless a greater number be specified. It is held to represent a spur-rowel and is the *cadency* mark for a third son.

MULLET PIERCED A *mullet, pierced* in the centre to show the *tincture* of the *field* on which it is borne.

MURAL CROWN A *crown* or *coronet* resembling a battlemented wall.

MURREY Mulberry colour, a rare *tincture*.

NAIANT Descriptive of a fish swimming in a horizontal position.

NAIANT CONTRA-NAIANT Two or more fish depicted swimming *dexter*wise and *sinister*wise alternately.

NAISSANT Rising, or coming out of; usually applied to animals emerging from a *fess* or other *ordinary*.

NAVAL CROWN A *crown* composed of the sterns and masts (with square-sails set) of ships set alternately on a circlet.

NEBULY A line of partition intended to represent clouds (see illustration on page 130).

NERVED Descriptive of leaves of plants when the veins are of a different *tincture* from the rest of the leaf.

NIMBATE Haloed.

NIMBUS A halo.

NOMBRIL POINT The point of a *shield* between *fess* point and middle *fess* point.

NOWED Knotted.

NOWY A partition line containing a semi-circular bulge.

OCTOFOIL An eight-lobed leaf.

OGRESS A pellet.

OPINICUS An heraldic monster with the head and neck of an *eagle,* the body and legs of a *lion* and the tail of a camel. It is also found with an *eagle's* wings.

OPPRESSED See *debruised.*

OR Gold or yellow.

ORB See *mound.*

ORDINARIES The ordinaries are the *bend, chevron, chief, cross, fess, pale, pall, pile* and *saltire.*

ORLE A diminutive of the *bordure,* but detached from the outer edge of the *shield. Charges* arranged in such a fashion are *blazoned* as 'in orle'.

OUNCE In heraldry synonymous with the *leopard.*

OVER ALL Descriptive of a *charge* or *ordinary* placed over other bearings.

OVERT Applied to the wings of birds when open for flight.

OWL Always drawn full faced but with the body *dexter*wise.

PALE An *ordinary* consisting of a band placed vertically in the middle of the *shield.*

PALE, IN Descriptive of two or more *charges* placed in the position of a *pale.*

PALE, PER Descriptive of a *shield* divided vertically in the centre.

PALEWISE Descriptive of a *charge* or *charges* placed erect.

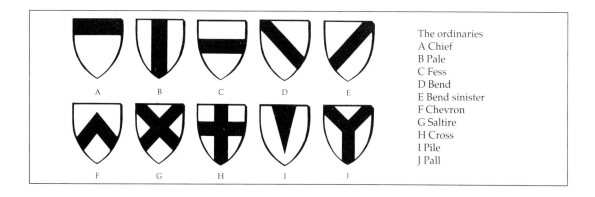

The ordinaries
A Chief
B Pale
C Fess
D Bend
E Bend sinister
F Chevron
G Saltire
H Cross
I Pile
J Pall

PALISADO A *crown* or *coronet* composed of palisade-shaped points set on a circlet.

PALL The heraldic representation of the pallium, the vestment peculiar to archbishops, in whose arms it occurs.

PALLET A diminutive of the *pale*.

PALY Descriptive of a *field* or *charge* divided into an equal number of pieces of alternate *tinctures* by vertical lines of partition.

PALY BENDY A combination of lines *per pale* and per *bend* forming *lozenges* of a peculiar shape (see illustration on page 129).

PALY BENDY SINISTER The above arrangement in reverse (see illustration on page 129).

PANACHE A triple row of plumes, much used as a *crest* in Continental heraldry.

PANTHER The heraldic panther is always depicted breathing fire.

PARTED Divided by.

PASCHAL LAMB A lamb *passant, nimbate,* and carrying over its right shoulder a staff topped with a *cross,* attached to which is a flowing *banner* charged with the Cross of St George.

PASSANT Walking; applied to all animals (except deer) shown walking from *sinister* to *dexter.*

PASSANT COUNTER PASSANT Two animals placed one above the other and walking in opposite directions.

PASSANT GUARDANT An animal walking with its head full face to the viewer.

PASSANT REGARDANT An animal walking with its head looking back.

PASSANT REPASSANT See *passant counter passant.*

PASSION CROSS See *calvary cross.*

PAVILION An oblong tent with a projecting entrance.

PEAN An heraldic fur represented as black with gold ermine spots.

PEGASUS A winged horse.

PELICAN IN HER PIETY This *charge* always depicts a pelican with wings *addorsed* and neck

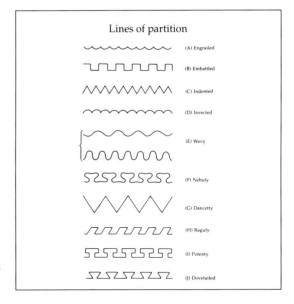

Lines of partition

(A) Engrailed
(B) Embattled
(C) Indented
(D) Invected
(E) Wavy
(F) Nebuly
(G) Dancetty
(H) Raguly
(I) Potenty
(J) Dovetailed

embowed, standing on her nest and pecking her breast, from which drops of blood flow to feed her young.

PELLET See *ogress.*

PELLETTY (or PELLETTÉE) Strewn with *pellets.*

PENDANT Hanging.

PENNER (sometimes PENNA) AND INKHORN A pencase with inkhorn or inkbottle attached thereto by a cord.

PENNANT A long, tapering, narrow *banner.*

PHEON The steel or iron head of a dart or arrow.

PHOENIX A fabulous bird, always depicted rising from flames.

PIERCED Applied to any *ordinary* or *charge* when perforated to show the *tincture* of the *field,* or any other specified *tincture.*

PILE An *ordinary* shaped like a wedge issuing from the *chief* and tapering towards the *base.*

PLATE A white or silver *roundle.*

PLENITUDE Descriptive of the full moon.

PLUME A plume in heraldry generally consists of three ostrich feathers.

POING A closed hand, in contradistinction to *appaumy.*

POMME A green *roundle*.

POMMEL The rounded knob at the top of the handle of a sword or dagger.

POPINJAY A small parrot with green plumage and red beak and legs.

PORTANT Descriptive of a *cross* which is not erect but placed athwart the *shield* as though carried on a shoulder.

PORTCULLIS The grille which may be lowered over the gateway of a town or castle for defence purposes. Heraldically it is usually represented by a square of latticed metal work with the vertical bars terminating in points at the bottom and with chains attached to the sides at the top.

POTENTY (in older *blazons* POTENTÉ) A line of division formed by a succession of crutch-shaped figures.

POULDRON Shoulder armour.

POUNCE The talons of a bird of prey.

POWDERED Descriptive of a *field* strewn with minor *charges* synonymous with *semy*.

PREYING Descriptive of a bird or animal standing on and devouring its prey.

PROPER A *charge* is so described when shown in its natural colour or colours.

PURPURE Purple.

PYTHON In heraldry a winged serpent.

QUARTERING The division of a *shield* into four quarters, each bearing different arms. The quarterings may be quartered in their turn and there is really no limit to the number of arms exhibited if it is desired to show all those to which an individual may be entitled through descent from *armigerous* heiresses.

QUATREFOIL A four-lobed leaf or petal.

QUEUE The tail of an animal.

QUEUE-FOURCHÉE A forked tail.

QUINTAIN A tilting post.

RADIATED Rayed.

RAGGED Descriptive of a roughly trimmed treetrunk.

RAGGED STAFF, BEAR AND The *badge* of the Dudleys.

RAGULY Descriptive of the stylized version of *ragged*.

RAMPANT The most common position in heraldry. An animal is described as rampant when depicted standing on one hind leg (normally the left) with the other slightly raised in front and the forepaws also stretched out. The tail is curved up over the back.

REFLEXED or REFLECTED Applied to chains attached to the collars of animals when they are thrown over the back.

REGUARDANT Looking backwards.

RERE MOUSE A bat.

RESPECTING Descriptive of two animals face to face.

RETORTED Descriptive of serpents wreathed together.

RIBAND or RIBBON One-eighth part of a *bend*.

RISING Descriptive of birds about to take flight.

ROMPU Broken.

ROSE A very common *charge*. The heraldic rose has five petals and a large centre, with short, pointed leaves issuing from between the petals.

ROSE-EN-SOLEIL A white heraldic *rose* in the centre of a golden-rayed sun.

ROUNDLE A round plate or disc of various *tinctures*, eg *bezant, golpe, hurt*.

RUSTRE A *lozenge* pierced by a round hole.

SABLE Black; abbreviated to sa.

SAGITTARIUS See *centaur*.

SALAMANDER A fabulous reptile, represented as a lizard surrounded by flames.

SALIENT Descriptive of an animal springing.

SALTIRE A diagonal *cross* with arms extending to the edges of the *shield*.

SALTIRE COUPED A diagonal *cross* with the arms terminating short of the edge of the *shield*.

SANG Blood.

SANGLIER A wild boar.

SANGUINE Blood colour.

SARACEN'S HEAD See *Moor's head*.

SARCELLE Cut through the middle.

SCALLOPED Scaled with even, semi-circular scales as opposed to triangular, fish-tailed, oval, or other shapes.

SCARPE A diminutive of the *bend sinsister*, one-half its width.

SCINTILLANT Sparkling.

SCROLL or ESCROLL The *band* on which the *motto* is placed, usually beneath the *shield*.

SEA MONSTERS Mythological creatures, such as the sea ape, sea bear, sea bull, sea cat, sea dog, sea dragon, sea horse, sea lion, sea stag, are usually depicted with the foreparts of the land animals and the tails of fishes.

SEAX A scimitar with a semi-circular notch in the back of the blade.

SEGREANT Applied to a *griffin* in the *rampant* position.

SEJANT Seated.

SEJANT ERECT Descriptive of a *sejant lion* with raised forelegs.

SEMY (in older *blazons* SEMÉE) *Powdered*.

SERRATED Indented or cut like a saw.

SEXFOIL A flower with six leaves.

SHAKEFORK Similar to the *pall*, but not touching the edges of the *shield*.

SHAMROCK A *trefoil*.

SHEAF See *garb*.

SHIELD The shield which bears the actual arms forms the main part of all *achievements*. There are many shapes, but in general it resembles an inverted triangle springing from the base of a rectangle.

SINISTER The left-hand side of the *shield*, which is the right side to the observer.

SINOPLE Green in French heraldry.

SLIPPED Applied to flowers and leaves when depicted with a piece of stalk attached.

SPHINX A mythical animal with the head and breast of a woman, the body of a *lion*, and the wings of an *eagle*.

SPLENDOUR, IN A term applied to the sun when depicted with a human face and environed by rays.

STAR See *estoile* and *mullet*.

STATANT Standing.

STREWED See *powdered* and *semy*.

STRINGED Applied to the cords of bows, harps, hunting-horns, etc.

SUB-ORDINARIES Diminutives of the *ordinaries*, comprising the *bordure, canton, flaunche, fret, gyron, inescutcheon, orle, pile* and *tressure*

SUFFLUE A rest or *clarion*.

SUPPORTERS Human or animal figures placed on either side of a *shield* as though supporting it. Supporters are only borne by members of the royal family, peers, Knights Grand Cross of Orders of Knighthood, and certain *baronets*, corporate bodies and others to whom they may have been granted as a special honour.

SURCOAT A sleeveless coat, worn over body armour and usually displaying the wearer's arms.

SURGEANT Rising (as applied to birds).

SURMOUNTED Descriptive of one *charge* placed upon another.

SURTOUT or SUR-LE-TOUT An *escutcheon* placed upon the centre of a *shield* is sometimes so described.

SYKE A fountain; used in the *canting* arms of Sykes.

TABARD The *surcoat* worn by heralds and pursuivants.

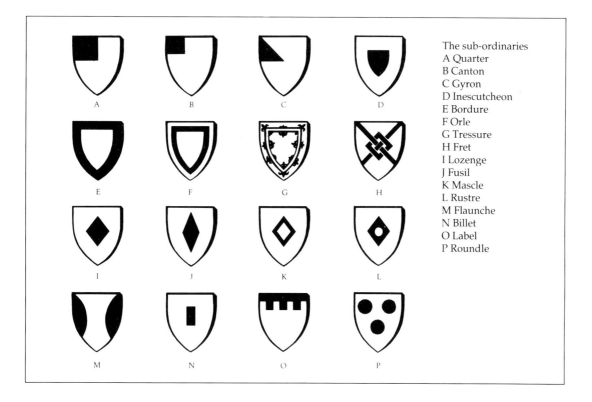

The sub-ordinaries
A Quarter
B Canton
C Gyron
D Inescutcheon
E Bordure
F Orle
G Tressure
H Fret
I Lozenge
J Fusil
K Mascle
L Rustre
M Flaunche
N Billet
O Label
P Roundle

TABERNACLE A tent or *pavilion*.

TALBOT A hound or hunting-dog.

TALENT See *bezant*.

TARGE or TARGET A circular *shield*.

TASCES or TASSES Thigh armour.

TAU CROSS A *cross* shaped like the Greek letter tau.

TENNÉ or TAWNY Orange colour.

THISTLE Always depicted with two leaves attached to the stalk. It is the emblem of Scotland.

THUNDERBOLT Depicted as a twisted *bar* in *pale*, inflamed at each end and surmounting two jagged darts in *saltire* between two wings *expanded* with streams of fire issuing from the centre.

TIARA The papal triple-*crown*, depicted as a conical cap topped with an *orb* and *cross* and encircled by three *coronets*.

TIERCE Descriptive of a *shield* divided into three equal parts of different *tinctures*.

TINCTURES The heraldic term for colours (see main text, page 22).

TORQUED Wreathed.

TORSE The *wreath* upon which the *crest* is placed.

TORTEAU A red *roundle*.

TORTILLÉ A French term for *nowed*, twisted, or *wreathed*.

TRANSFIXED Pierced through.

TREFOIL A three-lobed leaf.

TRESSURE A double inner border. In an *impaled* coat it does not run down the line of the *pale*.

TRICK The system of depicting a coat of arms when colours are not used but indicated by a form of heraldic shorthand.

TRICORPORATE Descriptive of the bodies of three animals depicted issuing from the *dexter*, *sinister* and *base* points of the *shield* and meeting *conjoined* to one head in the centre.

TRIPPANT The term applied to stags and similar animals of the deer variety, corresponding to *passant*. Two animals tripping past each other in opposite directions are described as counter-trippant.

TRIUMPHAL CROWN A laurel *wreath*.

TRUE LOVERS' KNOT An elaborate double knot from which the arms of unmarried ladies are sometimes suspended.

TUDOR ROSE A double *rose* representing the union of the white and red *rose* emblems of the rival houses of York and Lancaster following the marriage of Henry VII and Elizabeth of York.

TUN A large barrel.

TURNED UP Descriptive of the lining of a cap, etc, turned up over the edge.

TURRETED Descriptive of a wall or tower surmounted by small turrets.

UMBRACED See *vambraced*.

UNGULED Hooved.

UNICORN A fabulous animal resembling a horse with cloven hooves and a long twisted horn growing out of its forehead.

UNIFOIL A single-lobed leaf.

UPRIGHT Applied to reptiles and fish, as *rampant* is to animals.

URCHIN A hedgehog.

URINANT Descriptive of a fish swimming with its head downwards and tail erect; the opposite of *hauriant*.

VAIR An heraldic fur represented by rows of small *shields* alternately reversed.

VALLARY CROWN A *crown* composed of flat pointed strips mounted on a circlet.

VAMBRACED Descriptive of an arm covered in armour.

VAMPLATE A gauntlet.

VAMPLET A tilting spear.

VANNET An *escallop* represented without the two projecting ears.

VERDOY A border *charged* with eight flowers, leaves, fruit or vegetables.

VERT Green.

VESTED Clothed.

VISCOUNT The fourth rank in the peerage, between *earl* and *baron*. A viscount's *coronet* is composed of a gilt circlet, *chased as jewelled*, surmounted by sixteen silver balls, nine of which are shown when it is depicted heraldically.

VISCOUNTESS The wife of a *viscount* or a peeress in her own right.

VIZOR The raisable part of a *helmet* which can be lowered to protect the eyes.

VOIDED Descriptive of a *charge* when the centre has been cut out to leave a framework round the edge.

VOLANT Flying.

VULNED Wounded.

WATER BOUGET The bags or buckets in which water was carried, always depicted united by the yoke or crossbar, fashioned to pass over the shoulders.

WAVY A line of partition formed like waves.

WHIRLPOOL See *gorges*.

WILD MAN Usually depicted as a bearded man carrying a club and *wreathed* about the head and loins with foliage, but otherwise naked.

WOOD Represented in heraldry by a group of five or more trees.

WOUND A purple *roundle*; also known as a *golpe*.

WREATH A *garland*, *chaplet*, or attire for the head. A *crest* wreath, however, is usually composed of two bands of interwoven silk.

WYVERN An heraldic monster with the wings and upper part of a *dragon* and the lower part of the body tapering away into a barbed tail.

ZULE A *chess rook*.

The Existing Royal Regalia of England and Scotland

England

Unless otherwise stated all the items listed are kept in the Jewel House at the Tower of London, which is open to the public.

1 St Edward's Crown

The coronation crown made for King Charles II in 1661 and said to contain fragments of the crown broken up under the Commonwealth in 1649. It has been used as the actual coronation crown of all succeeding sovereigns except Mary II, George IV, Victoria and Edward VII.

2 The Imperial State Crown

This crown was originally made for Queen Victoria in 1838 and used as her actual coronation crown. It was also used as the coronation crown of King Edward VII, St Edward's Crown being considered too heavy for him to wear in his convalescent condition. It was remodelled for King George VI and again for the present Queen and is worn annually at the State Opening of Parliament.

3 The Imperial Crown of India

This very elegant crown was made for King George V to wear at the Delhi Durbar in 1911, after it had been discovered that the law forbade any of the existing crowns to be taken out of this country. It has never been used since.

4 Mary of Modena's Diadem

A diadem of gold set with diamonds in openwork silver settings and surmounted with pearls. It was made for James II's consort to wear on her way to the Abbey and until her crowning, and was similarly used by subsequent queen consorts, the last being Queen Adelaide in 1831.

5 Mary of Modena's Coronation Crown

Made for the coronation of James II's Queen and subsequently used, with one of the arches detached, by the future George II as Prince of Wales at the coronation of his father George I. In its original form it was again used as the coronation crown of Caroline of Ansbach, consort of George II. Originally set with diamonds, it was later reset with pastes and is now in the Museum of London.

6 Mary of Modena's State Crown

A very pretty little crown made for James II's consort to wear on her return from the Abbey and throughout the Coronation Banquet. It was possibly used as the coronation crown of Queen Mary II.

7 Queen Victoria's small diamond crown

This was made at her own expense in 1870 for the Queen to wear on state occasions and is familiar from many portraits and photographs. It was later worn by Queen Alexandra at State Openings of Parliament and was deposited in the Tower of London by King George VI on his accession.

8 Queen Alexandra's Crown

Made for the coronation of Edward VII's consort in 1902, subsequently reset with paste and presented by her to the London Museum (now the Museum of London).

9 Queen Mary's Crown

Made for the coronation of George V's consort in 1911. The Koh-i-Noor and two of the lesser Stars of Africa diamonds have been replaced by crystals. Queen Mary wore it with the arches detached at the coronation of King George VI in 1937.

10 Queen Elizabeth The Queen Mother's Crown

Made for the coronation of George VI's consort in 1937 and again worn by her, with the arches detached, at the coronation of Queen Elizabeth II in 1953.

11 The Prince of Wales's Crowns

The first of these was made to be carried before Frederick, Prince of Wales, son of George II, when attending State Openings of Parliament and was apparently never worn. A crown of very similar design appears in a portrait of the Prince's mother, Caroline of Ansbach, which depicts her in the robes worn at the coronation of her father-in-law, King George I, and also in state portraits of Frederick's widow, Augusta. The second crown was made for the future King George V to wear at the coronation of his father King Edward VII in 1902 and was also worn by his son, the future Edward VIII, in 1911.

12 Edward, Prince of Wales's Crown

A light circlet without an arch used at the investiture of Edward, Prince of Wales (subsequently King Edward VIII and Duke of Windsor), at Caernarvon Castle in 1911 and now in the National Museum of Wales at Cardiff.

13 Charles, Prince of Wales's Crown

A very modern interpretation of a single-arched crown made for the investiture of HRH The Prince of Wales at Caernarvon Castle in 1969 and now in the National Museum of Wales at Cardiff.

(The Museum of London possesses on loan the crown-frames for the State Crowns of George I and George IV, the Crown of Queen Adelaide, and the original frame of Queen Victoria's State Crown, which was reset in an identical frame in 1937.)

14 The Sceptre with the Cross

Made for Charles II, it had the largest Star of Africa, reputedly the largest diamond in the world, set in its head in 1907.

15 The Sceptre with the Dove (also known as the Rod of Equity and Mercy)

Made for Charles II's coronation and used at every subsequent coronation.

16 The Queen's Sceptre with the Cross

Made for the coronation of Mary of Modena, James II's Queen, and used at all subsequent coronations of consorts.

17 The Queen's Ivory Rod

Made for Mary of Modena's coronation in 1685 and used (as her Sceptre with the Dove) at the coronation of Queen Mary II and at all subsequent coronations of consorts.

18 St Edward's Staff

The provenance and use of this interesting item of regalia are discussed in the main text (page 79).

19 The Orb

Made for the coronation of Charles II and further embellished for later sovereigns.

20 Queen Mary II's Orb

Made for the coronation of William and Mary as joint sovereigns in 1689; queen consorts are not invested with an orb in England. In 1901 both Orbs were placed on Queen Victoria's coffin for her funeral procession, the 'Queen's Orb', the smaller one, being said to represent the Empire of India.

21 The three Swords of State

(a) *Curtana* (the Sword of Mercy), which has the top broken off. (b) The Jewelled Sword of Offering, with which the sovereign is girded and subsequently offers at the altar, made for the coronation of George IV and used at all subsequent coronations. (c) The Great Sword of State, borne before the sovereign on state occasions.

22 The Golden Spurs

A male sovereign's heels are touched with these before the girding with the sword; a female sovereign merely lays her hand upon them before they are returned to the altar.

23 The Armills (or Bracelets)

There are two sets of these. (a) A gold and enamel pair made for the coronation of King Charles II. (b) A gold pair made for the coronation of Queen Elizabeth II in 1953 and presented by the governments of the United Kingdom, Canada, Australia, New Zealand, Ceylon, Pakistan, South Africa and Southern Rhodesia.

24 The Coronation Rings

There are three of these. (a) The Sovereign's Ring, bearing the cross of St George in rubies across a sapphire, made for the coronation of King William IV and used at the coronation of King Edward VII and all subsequent coronations. (b) The Queen Consort's Ring, a ruby surrounded by diamonds, made for the coronation of Queen Adelaide and used at all subsequent coronations of consorts. (c) A smaller version of the Sovereign's Ring made for Queen Victoria, at whose coronation the Archbishop insisted on forcing it on the wrong finger much to her discomfort and annoyance.

25 The Ampulla and Anointing Spoon

The only two items in the regalia which survived the destruction under the Commonwealth. The Ampulla dates from the late fourteenth century and the spoon from the late twelfth century (see page 78–9)

Scotland

The Scottish regalia, the oldest in the British Isles, are on public view in the Crown Room at Edinburgh Castle.

1 The Crown

This extremely elegant crown is a masterpiece of the Renaissance jewellers' art. It was made for King James V and is believed to incorporate material from earlier crowns, including that of Robert the Bruce. It was used symbolically at the coronation of the infant Mary in 1542 and at the coronations of James VI, Charles I and Charles II. Lost sight of for many years, it was rediscovered by Sir Walter Scott and borne in front of George IV on his famous visit to Edinburgh in 1822. It was last used on 24 June 1953 when the 'Honours of Scotland' (the regalia) were delivered to Queen Elizabeth II at a service in St Giles's Cathedral, Edinburgh.

2 The Sceptre

Of Italian workmanship, the sceptre was presented to King James IV by Pope Alexander VI in 1494.

3 The Sword of State

Another piece of Italian workmanship, presented to King James IV by Pope Julius II in 1507. The Pope's name is etched in gold on either side of the blade.

4 The Ring

A ruby ring, allegedly the coronation ring of King Charles I. It was carried into exile by James II (VII of Scotland) in 1688 and bequeathed to George III by Cardinal York in 1807.

APPENDIX 3

The Coronations of British Sovereigns

1 Coronations before the Conquest

There are few specific references to coronations or inauguration rites of the early Anglo-Saxon kings, but the kings of Wessex were installed on the ancient Kings' Stone, which still stands near the parish church at Kingston-upon-Thames, Surrey.

Date of Coronation	Person Crowned	Place of Coronation	Prelate or other Officiant
? 871	Alfred the Great	Kingston or Winchester	?Ethelred, Archbishop of Canterbury
8 June 900	Edward the Elder	Kingston	Plegmund, Archbishop of Canterbury
5 Sept 925	Athelstan	Kingston	?Wulfhelm, Archbishop of Canterbury
16 Nov 940	Edmund I	Kingston	Oda, Archbishop of Canterbury
? Jan 956	Edwy	Kingston	Oda, Archbishop of Canterbury
11 May 973	Edgar and Elfrida	Bath Abbey	Dunstan, Archbishop of Canterbury and Oswald, Archbishop of York
? July 975	Edward the Martyr	Kingston	Dunstan, Archbishop of Canterbury
14 Apr 979	Ethelred II	Kingston	Dunstan, Archbishop of Canterbury
? Apr 1016	Edmund II Ironside	St Paul's Cathedral	?
6 Jan 1017	Canute	St Paul's Cathedral	?
? 1037	Harold I Harefoot	Oxford	?
18 June 1040	Hardicanute	Canterbury	Eadsige, Archbishop of Canterbury
3 Apr 1043	Edward the Confessor	Winchester Cathedral	Eadsige, Archbishop of Canterbury and Ethelric, Archbishop of York

| ? Jan 1045 | Edith (wife of Edward the Confessor) | Winchester Cathedral | Eadsige, Archbishop of Canterbury |
| 6 Jan 1066 | Harold II | Westminster Abbey | Stigand, Archbishop of Canterbury |

2 Coronations since the Conquest

Date of Coronation	Person Crowned	Place of Coronation	Prelate or other Officiant
25 Dec 1066	William I the Conqueror	Westminster Abbey	Ealdred, Archbishop of York
11 May 1068	Matilda of Flanders (wife of William I)	Winchester Cathedral	Ealdred, Archbishop of York
26 Sept 1087	William II Rufus	Westminster Abbey	Lanfranc, Archbishop of Canterbury
5 Aug 1100	Henry I	Westminster Abbey	Maurice, Bishop of London
11 Nov 1100	Matilda of Scotland (1st wife of Henry I)	Westminster Abbey	Anselm, Archbishop of Canterbury
3 Feb 1122	Adeliza of Louvain (2nd wife of Henry I)	Westminster Abbey	Ralph d'Escures, Archbishop of Canterbury
26 Dec 1135	Stephen	Westminster Abbey	William de Corbeil, Archbishop of Canterbury
22 March 1136	Matilda of Boulogne (wife of Stephen)	Westminster Abbey	William de Corbeil, Archbishop of Canterbury
(25 Dec 1141	Stephen said to have been recrowned)		
19 Dec 1154	Henry II	Westminster Abbey	Theobald, Archbishop of Canterbury
25 Dec 1158	Eleanor of Aquitaine (wife of Henry II)	Worcester Cathedral	Theobald, Archbishop of Canterbury
14 Jun 1170	Henry 'the Young King' (son and heir of Henry II)	Westminster Abbey	Roger of Pont l'Eveque, Archbishop of Canterbury
27 Aug 1172	Henry 'the Young King' recrowned with his wife Margaret of France	Winchester Cathedral	Rotrou, Archbishop of Rouen
3 Sept 1189	Richard I	Westminster Abbey	Baldwin, Archbishop of Canterbury
12 May 1191	Berengaria of Navarre (wife of Richard I)	Chapel of St George, Lemesos, Cyprus	John FitzLuke, Bishop of Evreux
27 May 1199	John	Westminster Abbey	Hubert Walter, Archbishop of Canterbury

8 Oct 1200	Isabella of Angoulême (wife of John)	Westminster Abbey	Hubert Walter, Archbishop of Canterbury
28 Oct 1216	Henry III	Gloucester Cathedral	Peter des Roches, Bishop of Winchester
17 May 1220	Henry III (recrowned)	Westminster Abbey	Stephen Langton, Archbishop of Canterbury
20 Jan 1236	Eleanor of Provence (wife of Henry III)	Westminster Abbey	Edmund Rich, Archbishop of Canterbury
19 Aug 1274	Edward I and Eleanor of Castile	Westminster Abbey	Edward Kilwardby, Archbishop of Canterbury
25 Feb 1308	Edward II and Isabelle of France	Westminster Abbey	Henry Merewell (alias Woodlock), Bishop of Winchester
1 or 2 Feb 1327	Edward III	Westminster Abbey	Walter Reynolds, Archbishop of Canterbury
20 Feb 1328	Philippa of Hainault (wife of Edward III)	Westminster Abbey	Simon Meopham, Archbishop of Canterbury
16 July 1377	Richard II	Westminster Abbey	Simon Sudbury, Archbishop of Canterbury
22 Jan 1382	Anne of Bohemia (1st wife of Richard II)	Westminster Abbey	William Courtenay, Archbishop of Canterbury
8 Jan 1397	Isabelle of France (2nd wife of Richard II)	Westminster Abbey	Thomas Arundel, Archbishop of Canterbury
13 Oct 1399	Henry IV	Westminster Abbey	Thomas Arundel, Archbishop of Canterbury
26 Feb 1403	Joan of Navarre (2nd wife of Henry IV)	Westminster Abbey	Thomas Arundel, Archbishop of Canterbury
9 April 1413	Henry V	Westminster Abbey	Thomas Arundel, Archbishop of Canterbury
24 Feb 1421	Catherine of France (wife of Henry V)	Westminster Abbey	Henry Chichele, Archbishop of Canterbury
6 Nov 1429	Henry VI	Westminster Abbey	Henry Chichele, Archbishop of Canterbury
30 May 1445	Margaret of Anjou (wife of Henry VI)	Westminster Abbey	John Stafford, Archbishop of Canterbury
29 June 1461	Edward IV	Westminster Abbey	Cardinal Bourchier, Archbishop of Canterbury
26 May 1465	Elizabeth Woodville (wife of Edward IV)	Westminster Abbey	Cardinal Bourchier, Archbishop of Canterbury
6 July 1483	Richard III and Anne Neville	Westminster Abbey	Cardinal Bourchier, Archbishop of Canterbury

30 Oct 1485	Henry VII	Westminster Abbey	Cardinal Bourchier, Archbishop of Canterbury
24 Nov 1487	Elizabeth of York (wife of Henry VII)	Westminster Abbey	John Morton, Archbishop of Canterbury
24 June 1509	Henry VIII and Catherine of Aragon	Westminster Abbey	William Warham, Archbishop of Canterbury
1 June 1533	Anne Boleyn (2nd wife of Henry VIII)	Westminster Abbey	Thomas Cranmer, Archbishop of Canterbury
20 Feb 1547	Edward VI	Westminster Abbey	Thomas Cranmer, Archbishop of Canterbury
1 Oct 1553	Mary I	Westminster Abbey	Stephen Gardiner, Bishop of Winchester
15 Jan 1559	Elizabeth I	Westminster Abbey	Owen Oglethorpe, Bishop of Carlisle
25 July 1603	James I and Anne of Denmark	Westminster Abbey	John Whitgift, Archbishop of Canterbury
2 Feb 1626	Charles I	Westminster Abbey	George Abbot, Archbishop of Canterbury
23 April 1661	Charles II	Westminster Abbey	William Juxon, Archbishop of Canterbury
23 April 1685	James II and Mary of Modena	Westminster Abbey	William Sancroft, Archbishop of Canterbury
11 April 1689	William III and Mary II (joint sovereigns)	Westminster Abbey	Henry Compton, Bishop of London
23 April 1702	Anne	Westminster Abbey	Thomas Tenison, Archbishop of Canterbury
20 Oct 1714	George I	Westminster Abbey	Thomas Tenison, Archbishop of Canterbury
11 Oct 1727	George II and Caroline of Brandenburg-Ansbach	Westminster Abbey	William Wake, Archbishop of Canterbury
22 Sept 1761	George III and Charlotte of Mecklenburg-Strelitz	Westminster Abbey	Thomas Secker, Archbishop of Canterbury
19 July 1821	George IV	Westminster Abbey	Charles Manners Sutton, Archbishop of Canterbury
8 Sept 1831	William IV and Adelaide of Saxe-Meiningen	Westminster Abbey	William Howley, Archbishop of Canterbury
28 June 1838	Victoria	Westminster Abbey	William Howley, Archbishop of Canterbury

9 Aug 1902	Edward VII and Alexandra of Denmark	Westminster Abbey	Frederick Temple, Archbishop of Canterbury William Dalrymple Maclagan, Archbishop of York
22 June 1911	George V and Mary of Teck	Westminster Abbey	Randall Thomas Davidson, Archbishop of Canterbury
12 May 1937	George VI and Elizabeth Bowes-Lyon	Westminster Abbey	Cosmo Gordon Lang, Archbishop of Canterbury
2 June 1953	Elizabeth II	Westminster Abbey	Geoffrey Francis Fisher, Archbishop of Canterbury

3 Scottish Coronations

From a very early period the Scottish kings were crowned or installed at Scone, taking their seat upon the 'Stone of Destiny' which Fergus Mor MacErc is said to have brought with him from Ireland towards the end of the fourth century. There are no detailed records of Scottish coronations before Malcolm III.

Date of Coronation	Person Crowned	Place of Coronation	Prelate or other Officiant
25 April 1058	Malcolm III	Scone	?
? Nov 1093	Donald Bane	Scone	?
? May 1094	Duncan II	Scone	?
? 1097	Edgar	Scone	?
? Jan 1107	Alexander I	Scone	?
? May 1124	David I	Scone	?
Summer 1153	Malcolm IV	Scone	?
24 Dec 1165	William the Lion	Scone	Richard, Bishop of St Andrews
6 Dec 1214	Alexander II	Scone	William Malvoisine, Bishop of St Andrews
13 July 1249	Alexander III	Scone	David de Bernham, Bishop of St Andrews
30 Nov 1292	John Balliol	Scone	?
27 March 1306	Robert I	Scone	Isabella, Countess of Buchan
24 Nov 1331	David II and Joan of England	Scone	James Bennet, Bishop of St Andrews
24 Sept 1332	Edward Balliol	Scone	?
26 March 1371	Robert II	Scone	William de Laundels, Bishop of St Andrews

? 1372	Euphemia Ross (2nd wife of Robert II)	Scone	Alexander de Kyninmund II, Bishop of Aberdeen
14 Aug 1390	Robert III and Annabella Drummond	Scone	Alexander de Neville, Bishop of St Andrews
21 May 1424	James I and Joan Beaufort	Scone	Henry Wardlaw, Bishop of St Andrews
25 March 1437	James II	Holyrood	Michael Ochiltree, Bishop of Dunblane
3 July 1449	Marie of Gueldres (wife of James II)	Holyrood	James Kennedy, Bishop of St Andrews
10 Aug 1460	James III	Kelso Abbey	James Kennedy, Bishop of St Andrews
13 July 1469	Margaret of Denmark (wife of James III)	Holyrood	Patrick Graham, Archbishop of St Andrews
26 June 1488	James IV	Scone	William Scheves, Archbishop of St Andrews
8 Aug 1503	Margaret Tudor (wife of James IV)	Holyrood	
21 Sept 1513	James V	Stirling	?
22 Feb 1540	Mary of Guise (2nd wife of James V)	Holyrood	Cardinal Beaton, Archbishop of St Andrews
9 Sept 1543	Mary	Stirling	Cardinal Beaton, Archbishop of St Andrews
29 July 1567	James VI	Stirling	Gavin Hamilton, Archbishop of St Andrews
17 May 1590	Anne of Denmark (wife of James VI)	Holyrood	?
18 June 1633	Charles I	Edinburgh	John Spottiswoode, Archbishop of St Andrews
1 Jan 1651	Charles II	Scone	Archibald Douglas, Earl of Angus

The titular King James VIII is said to have been crowned at Scone in Sept 1715, but no details of the ceremony are known.

Royal Regalia Worldwide

This list is not exhaustive, but includes most of the principal items of regalia still in existence and on public exhibition throughout the world.

Austria

The Imperial Crown of Austria was the magnificent crown made for the Holy Roman Emperor Rudolph II (1576–1612); the Imperial Sceptre, its shaft fashioned from a narwhal's horn and topped by a large sapphire, was made for his brother and successor Matthias (1612–1619); the Imperial Orb was also made for Matthias. These three items were adopted as the regalia of the Austrian Empire by Emperor Franz I in 1806, but never actually used as there was no coronation ceremony, although the Emperor was painted wearing them. The items are exhibited in the Kunsthistorisches Museum, Vienna.

Bavaria

The very elegant King's and Queen's Crowns, Sceptre and Orb were made in Paris by the goldsmith Biennais to the order of King Maximilian I when Bavaria became a kingdom in 1806. Their use was only symbolic, but the fact that King Ludwig II had the Queen's Crown altered for his fiancée Duchess Sophie suggests that she may have actually intended to wear it at her wedding had it ever taken place. Among other items, the Bavarian Treasury in Munich also possesses a very beautiful medieval crown, said to have been given by King Charles VI of France to his daughter Isabelle when she married King Richard II of England in 1396. After Richard's deposition it was appropriated by Henry IV, who gave it to his daughter Blanche on her marriage to the Elector Palatine. It was later worn by James I's daughter Elizabeth, the 'Winter Queen' of Bohemia.

Bohemia

The so-called Crown of St Wenceslas was made to the order of the Holy Roman Emperor Charles IV (1347–1378), who decreed that it should rest on the reliquary of St Wenceslas and only be removed for coronations of kings of Bohemia. The centre cross contains an alleged relic of the Crown of Thorns. The Bohemian Orb and Sceptre were made for Emperor Rudolph II (1576–1612) in Benvenuto Cellini's workshop. The last Bohemian coronation was that of Emperor Ferdinand I of Austria and Empress Maria Anna on 7 September 1836.

Brazil

The Imperial Crown of Brazil is constructed from Brazilian gold and set with Brazilian diamonds and is rather ugly and ill proportioned. It was made for the coronation of Dom Pedro I at Rio de Janeiro on 1 December 1822 and again used at the coronation of his son Dom Pedro II on 18 July 1841. It is now on public view in the Museum of the Imperial Palace at Petrópolis in Brazil with other items of the Brazilian regalia.

Bulgaria

Photographs of the wedding of King Ferdinand of Bulgaria to Princess Eleonore Reuss in 1908 show her wearing a small version of the Bulgarian heraldic crown in diamonds. It is not known if this still exists.

Denmark

The Crown of King Christian IV (1588–1648) is a very beautiful construction of gold, decorated with jewels and enamel work, and is probably the last European crown not to be arched. King Frederik III (1648–1670) had a new set of regalia made to mark the constitutional change from elec-

Above: The magnificent Imperial Crown of Austria
made for the Holy Roman Emperor Rudolph II
(1576–1612), with the Sceptre and Orb made for his
successor Matthias (1612–1619). The shaft of the Sceptre
is formed from a narwhal's horn.

Left: The Crown of Württemberg, made for King
William I of Württemberg (1816–1864) in 1822. Now in
the Württembergisches Landesmuseum in Stuttgart, it
was displayed at the funeral of Duke Philipp Albrecht,
head of the royal house, in April 1975.

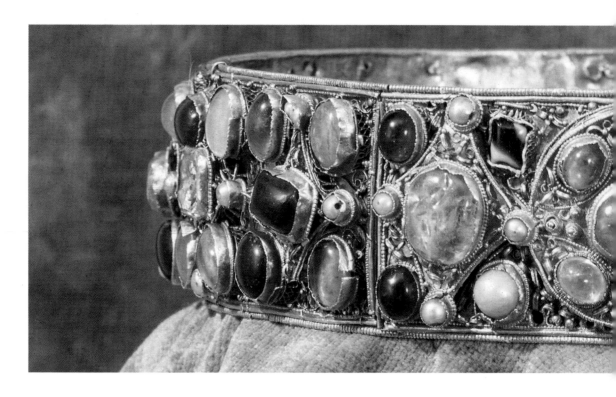

Above: The Crown of the Empress Kunigunde, wife of the Holy Roman Emperor Henry II, was probably made in Lorraine between 1010 and 1020. It is of gold and gold filigree and richly adorned with precious stones, pearls and glass pastes, although of the simple circlet type still then in vogue. The pious Empress later presented it to a monastery and it is now on display in the Treasury of the Residenz in Munich.

Opposite: This beautiful medieval crown may have been given by King Charles VI of France to his daughter Isabelle when she married King Richard II of England in 1396. It was later appropriated by King Henry IV, who included it in the dowry of his daughter Blanche when she married the Elector Palatine in 1402, and was worn by the famous 'Winter Queen' of Bohemia. It is now among the Bavarian state jewels on display in the Treasury of the Residenz in Munich.

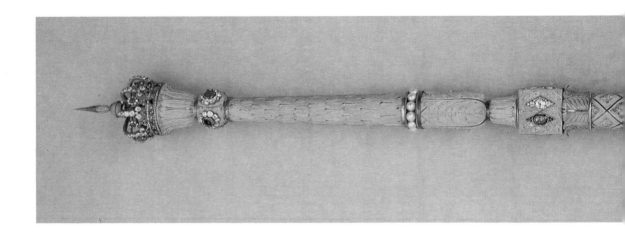

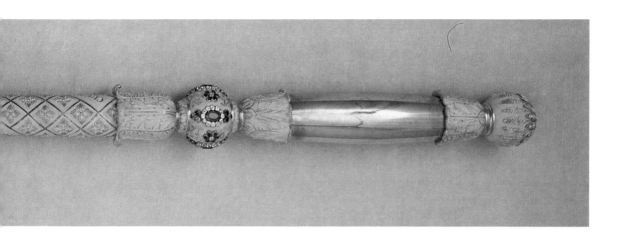

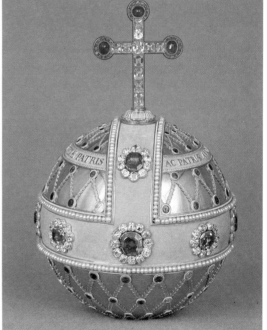

Above: The Bavarian King's Crown was made in Paris by Martin Guillaume Biennais (and his workshop) for King Max I Joseph in 1806. It is gold and parcel silver-gilt and set with brilliants, rubies, emeralds, sapphires and pearls.

Opposite: The Bavarian Queen's Crown was also made in Paris by Biennais in 1806 and altered by G Merk in 1867 at the order of King Ludwig II, who doubtless intended his fiancée, Duchess Sophie in Bavaria, to wear it at their wedding. In fact the engagement was broken off and the wedding never took place.

Above and top: The Bavarian Orb and Sceptre, part of the regalia made for Max I Joseph in 1806.

Emperor Haile Selassie I of Ethiopia and Empress Menen were photographed in their imperial crowns and robes following their coronation at St George's Cathedral, Addis Ababa, on 2 November 1930. The Emperor's crown is of very ancient design and allegedly based on that of King Solomon, from whose union with the Queen of Sheba the imperial family claim descent. The Empress's crown follows a more conventional European style.

tive to hereditary and absolute monarchy. The Crown was first used at the coronation of King Christian V in 1671. The last Danish coronation was that of King Christian VIII on 28 June 1840. The Danish regalia are on public display at Rosenborg Palace, Copenhagen.

Ethiopia

The crowns worn by the emperors of Ethiopia were high, castellated affairs similar to those depicted on ancient Assyrian monuments and somewhat reminiscent of the Papal Tiara. The crowns worn by the empresses were similar to the conventional European type of arched crown.

France

Most items of the French regalia were destroyed during the Revolution. Napoleon had a set of imperial regalia made for his coronation at Notre-Dame on 2 December 1804. He adopted several items from the old monarchy, most notably the Hand of Justice, a sceptre surmounted by a carved ivory hand. After the Restoration of the Bourbons a new set of regalia was made for the coronation of King Charles X at Rheims on 29 May 1825, the last French coronation. The 'citizen king' Louis Philippe had a crown made, but it was for symbolic display only. Various items of the French regalia are to be seen in the Louvre.

Germany

See 'Bavaria', 'Hanover', 'Prussia', 'Saxony' and 'Württemberg'.

Greece

A set of regalia for symbolic use was made for Otto of Bavaria when he was elected King of Greece in 1832 and he took it back to Bavaria with him when he went into exile in 1862. Nearly a hundred years later (1960) the House of Wittelsbach, in a generous gesture, presented the regalia to King Paul of the Hellenes in a ceremony at Athens. The kings of the house of Oldenburg also had some symbolic regalia made for display at oath-takings on accession and to surmount the coffin at royal funerals.

Hanover

The Hanoverian crown jewels disappeared mysteriously when Hanover was annexed to Prussia in 1866. The small diamond wedding crown made for the marriage of Queen Charlotte to King George III in 1761 is now at Windsor Castle and is traditionally lent for princesses of the royal house of Hanover to wear at their weddings.

Hawaii

In 1883 King Kalakaua of Hawaii determined on holding a coronation ceremony for himself and his Queen Kapiolani. A set of regalia was ordered from London and the coronation took place in a specially constructed pavilion in the grounds of the Iolani Palace in Honolulu. Queen Kapiolani's ladies had hastily to unpin her elaborate coiffeur when the impatient King came to set the crown on his wife's head and found it was too small. The crowns are now on public view at the Iolani Palace. Also to be reckoned as items of regalia are the *kahilis*, the long plumed staves carried before Hawaiian royalty on ceremonial occasions.

Holy Roman Empire

The crown of the Holy Roman Empire is the so-called Crown of Charlemagne, constructed from eight hinged gold plates richly adorned with jewels and enamel work. The central plate is surmounted by a cross from which a single arch springs to the back plate. The crown actually dates from the time of the Emperor Otto I (936–972), who was crowned by the Pope on 2 February 962. The arch was added by Emperor Otto III (983–1002). Several other crowns of Holy Roman Emperors and Empresses still exist, including that of Richard of Cornwall, King of the Romans (the brother of King Henry III of England), who was crowned as such at Aachen on 17 May 1257. His crown now surmounts the reliquary bust of Charlemagne in the Cathedral Treasury at Aachen.

Hungary

St Stephen's Crown is of Byzantine workmanship and according to tradition was presented to St Stephen I, Hungary's first king, by Pope Sylvester III in 1000. It has suffered many vicissitudes, including being crammed into a box too small to contain it, so that the cross surmounting it became bent to one side and has never been righted since. After a sojourn in Fort Knox following the Second World War, the Crown is now back in Budapest and is regarded as the symbol of Hungarian sovereignty. It was last used at the coronation of the Emperor Charles as King of Hungary at Budapest on 30 December 1916. The Hungarian Royal Sceptre also belonged to St Stephen and the crystal ball surmounting it is believed to be of Egyptian Muslim workmanship. The Royal Orb is a plain object of silver gilt surmounted by a double cross. It dates from the time of the Angevin Kings of Hungary in the late fourteenth century. The most magnificent item of the Hungarian regalia is the richly jewelled Apostolic Cross, another medieval piece, which was carried before the Hungarian sovereigns. The Hungarian Queen's Crown worn by the Empresses Elisabeth and Zita is of conventional design and looks top-heavy in the coronation photographs of the latter.

Iran

The magnificently jewelled crowns of the shahs of Iran and the crown made for the coronation of Empress Farah on 26 October 1967 were formerly on show to the public at the head office of the Bank of Iran, but it is not known what has become of them since the Revolution.

Italy

The crown of Italy, in so far as there is one, is the so-called Iron Crown of Lombardy, the core of which is alleged to have been a nail of the True Cross. Its early history is obscure; it became the crown of the kings of the Lombards and later figured in several imperial coronations, including that of Emperor Charles V at Bologna. Napoleon used it for his coronation as King of Italy at Milan on 26 May 1805.

Malaysia

Most of the Malaysian sultans possess crowns and other regalia. The crowns are of the usual European style with the Muslim symbol of the crescent substituted for the cross.

Nepal

The crown of the kings of Nepal is a richly bejewelled gold helmet with an aigrette or plume mounted in the centre. Very similar crowns are, or were, also worn by senior members of the Rana family, which provided prime ministers and dominated Nepalese politics for over a century from 1846 to 1950/1, when the royal authority was re-established.

Netherlands

The Dutch regalia, being intended for symbolic display only, are neither beautiful nor valuable. A set was made for the inauguration of King William I in 1815, but as he took it with him when he abdicated in 1840, his son King William II had a new crown, orb, sword and sceptre made for his inauguration. They are of silver gilt, set with imitation gems, and only appear at the inaugurations of the

Dutch sovereigns, when they are displayed on a table.

Norway
The existing Norwegian regalia were made for the coronation of Carl XIV Johan (Bernadotte) as King of Norway at Trondheim on 7 September 1818. The crown, similar in design to the Swedish ones, bears a very large Brazilian amethyst as its chief jewel. The sceptre and orb are of conventional design and the sword is that which Bernadotte carried at the Battle of Leipzig in 1813. Another item is the Anointing Horn, made to contain the oil used for the King's anointing. There are also a crown, orb and sceptre for the Queen, made for the coronation of Queen Désirée as Queen of Norway in 1830. The last Norwegian coronation was that of King Haakon VII and Queen Maud, the first King and Queen after Norway gained its independence from Sweden. They were crowned at Trondheim on 22 June 1906. Their son, King Olav V, merely received a blessing on 22 June 1958. The crown was displayed at his funeral in January 1991, and again at the solemn blessing of his son King Harald V and Queen Sonja at Trondheim on 23 June 1991.

Poland
The oldest existing item of the Polish regalia is the Coronation Sword, called *Szczerbiec* ('nicked'). It was made in Lorraine in the thirteenth century and has a steel blade and a gold and enamel hilt. It was first used as the Coronation Sword at the coronation of King Wladyslaw Lokietek on 20 January 1320. After the partition of Poland in 1795 it had a rather chequered history, travelling to Paris and St Petersburg, and only returning to Poland in 1924. Many sets of burial regalia have been retrieved from the graves of Polish kings and queens. Most of these may be seen in the National Museum in Warsaw, which also contains the regalia of King August III and Queen Maria Józefa, who were crowned on 17 January 1734. Their rather ugly crowns are set with jewels from the state treasury of Saxony, of which country August was also Elector.

Portugal
The last coronation to take place in Portugal was that of King John IV (the father of Charles II's Queen, Catherine of Bragança) at Lisbon on 15 December 1640. As an act of devotion, he placed his crown on the head of a statue of the Virgin and no subsequent monarch had the temerity to remove it to be crowned. Thereafter, each accession was marked by an 'acclamation', or presentation of the new sovereign for public approval, and an oath-taking. The royal family left Portugal in the face of Napoleon's invading armies in 1807 and went to Brazil, where the United Kingdom of Portugal, Brazil and the Algarves was proclaimed on 16 December 1815. The following year, on the accession of King John VI, it was decided to make the 'acclamation' an occasion of some ceremony and a new set of symbolic regalia was ordered. The crown and sceptre of Brazilian gold, unadorned by jewels, were made at Rio de Janeiro in 1817 and featured in the acclamation there on 6 February 1818. When King John VI returned to Portugal in 1821 he took the regalia with him and they were used in the accession ceremonies of his successors down to the last King Manuel II in 1908. The crown and sceptre may now be seen in the Palacio Nacional da Ajuda at Lisbon, together with the richly jewelled insignia of several Portuguese orders.

Prussia
The Prussian regalia were made for the coronation of King Frederick I at Königsberg on 18 January 1701 and used at all subsequent coronations until that of King William I on 18 October 1861. He was proclaimed German Emperor on 8 January 1871 and neither of his successors was crowned as King of Prussia. The crowns of the German emperor, empress and crown prince were heraldic designs only and never existed as artefacts, although Emperor William II had a new Prussian crown made in 1889 and liked to be photographed with it standing beside him on a table. The Prussian sceptre, part of the original regalia, is surmounted by a crowned eagle, studded with diamonds and having its body formed by a large garnet which was given to King Frederick I by Peter the Great of Russia. Items of the regalia are exhibited in the Charlottenburg Palace, near Berlin.

Romania
The Crown of Romania, although of conventional design, is unique in that it contains no precious metal and is unadorned with jewels or enamel work. It was fashioned from steel taken from one of the guns used at the Battle of Plevna in 1877

and was first used at the coronation of King Carol I at Bucharest on 22 May 1881. It was also used at the coronation of King Ferdinand I at Alba Julia on 15 October 1922 (the last coronation to take place in Continental Europe). Romania's two romantic queens, Elisabeth of Wied (Carmen Sylva) and Marie of Edinburgh, devised their own crowns, the former favouring a medieval type and the latter a Byzantine style.

Russia

The Russian regalia, containing some of the most opulent items of jewellery in the world, combine Eastern splendour with more Western elements to create a style which is unique. The domed crown known as the Crown of Vladimir Monomakh, may be of Byzantine origin and was certainly used for the coronation of Ivan the Terrible at Moscow in 1547, as it was for most of his successors until Peter the Great. Ivan also had several other crowns made for the lands he conquered – the Crown of Astrakhan, the Crown of Kazan, and so on. After Peter the Great proclaimed the Russian Empire in 1721, he had new regalia made for himself and for his wife Catherine, whom he crowned at Moscow in 1724. The items of the Russian regalia are displayed in the Kremlin at Moscow. The wedding crown, worn by Russian grand duchesses and constructed from a diamond-studded belt, is now in the United States.

Saxony

Although possessing some magnificent jewelled artefacts, the kings of Saxony do not appear to have had any items which might be classified as regalia.

Spain

The earliest items of Spanish regalia are the Visigothic crowns which were presented as votive offerings to hang in the Cathedral at Toledo. It is uncertain whether these were also the coronation crowns of the kings who donated them. The Kingdoms of Aragon and Navarre had a tradition of coronation, but Castile did not and it was the custom of Castile which was followed when Spain became united. However, a symbolic crown and sceptre were displayed at the ceremony of the sovereign taking the oath to the Constitution and last appeared at the oath-taking of King Juan Carlos I on 22 November 1975. The crown, a poor thing of

silver gilt, was made in 1775 by the Madrid silversmith Fernando Velasco and is completely unadorned with jewels. The sceptre dates from the seventeenth century and has a head of rock crystal. Queen Isabel II often wore a small crown similar to that worn by Queen Victoria, and King Alfonso XIII gave his wife, Queen Victoria Eugenia, a small crown which she wore on state occasions such as the opening of the Cortes.

Sweden

The Swedish royal regalia contain some of the most beautiful items of their genre. The oldest pieces which have survived are the two Swords of State which date from the time of Gustav Vasa. The oldest surviving crown was made by the Flemish goldsmith Cornelius ver Weiden for the coronation of King Eric XIV at Uppsala on 29 June 1561. The sceptre was also made in 1561 by Hans Heidenrik and further embellished in 1568, 1719 and 1780. The orb was made by Cornelius ver Weiden and had additions made to it by Frantz Beijer of Antwerp in 1568, being again altered in 1751. An item unique to Sweden is the Key of State, an ornate silver-gilt key. The earliest surviving queen's regalia are the sceptre and orb made for Gunilla Bielke, the second wife of King Johan III in 1585. The Anointing Horn was made for the coronation of King Carl IX in 1607 and is richly set with diamonds and rubies. The earliest queen's crown was made for the coronation of Maria Eleonora of Brandenburg, the consort of Gustavus Adolphus and mother of Queen Christina, by the German goldsmith Rupprecht Miller in 1620. It was used as the coronation crown of Queen Christina in 1650, and King Adolf Fredrik in 1751. Maria Eleonora's orb and sceptre were also the work of Rupprecht Miller. Another very elegant crown was made for Queen Lovisa Ulrika, the wife of King Adolf Fredrik in 1751. There are also several crowns made for princes and princesses of the royal family to wear at coronations and openings of Parliament. The last Swedish coronation was that of King Oscar II on 12 May 1873 and crowns continued to be worn at openings of Parliament until the end of his reign. Since then the items have had a symbolic use only. They are now displayed in the treasury of the Royal Palace at Stockholm. A far older Swedish crown, is that of the martyred King St Eric (d1160), which is preserved in his shrine in Uppsala Cathedral. It is a circlet of copper gilt, chased, and

King Peter of Serbia riding through the streets of Belgrade after his coronation on 21 September 1904. The ride must have been quite an ordeal for the sixty-year-old King as his crown, forged from gunmetal, weighed over 9 pounds (4kg).

decorated with semi-precious coloured stones. The treasury of Uppsala Cathedral also contains several crowns and other items of burial regalia removed from royal tombs.

Tahiti
The island of Tahiti in the South Pacific was a monarchy from 1773 until 1891 under the Pomare Dynasty. A crown of gilded metal with a red velvet cap is said to have been presented by the British government via the London Missionary Society to King Pomare III on the day of his coronation in 1824, although it is rather too large for a child of four. In appearance the crown is very reminiscent of a marquess's coronet and the word TAHITI is inscribed in relief on the rim. There are also a sceptre of turned wood surmounted by an eagle which is of uncertain date and origin, a ring of 22 carat gold with a carved carnelian, and a

sabre presented by Queen Victoria to Tamatoa V on the day of his coronation as King of Ra'iatea in 1857. The crown and sceptre are now in Le Musée de Tahiti et des Iles; the ring and sabre are in the possession of King Tamatoa V's great-grandson, Pomare Hitu Aitu Tom William Stevenson.

Thailand
The kings of Thailand possess a large and very varied regalia ranging from crowns, tall and pointed in shape, to tea-kettles, which play their part in court ceremonials and are carried in procession at royal cremations.

Tonga
The Crown of Tonga, reputedly the heaviest in the world, was made for King George Tupou II and used at the coronations of Queen Salote Tupou III (1918) and King Taufa'ahau Tupou IV (1968).

Württemberg
The elegant Crown of Württemberg, now in Stuttgart's Landesmuseum, was made in Stuttgart by August Heinrich Kuhn (1749–1827) in 1822/4 for King William I. It is of more delicate workmanship than the other German crowns, but was never worn, its use being purely symbolic.

Yugoslavia
The Crown of Yugoslavia was made for the coronation of King Peter I of Serbia at Belgrade on 21 September 1904, the only Serbian coronation to take place in modern times. It is of no great value, being made from gunmetal taken from a cannon which had been used in Karageorge's campaign against the Turks, but its general appearance is improved by gilt and enamel work. It weighs over 9 pounds (4kg) and the Austrian ambassador, who was present at King Peter's coronation, noted that the King 'was obliged to take off the crown from time to time during the service in the Cathedral'. According to an article in the *Sunday Telegraph* of 7 April 1991, the crown is 'in a cupboard at the moment' somewhere in Belgrade and 'not in a bad condition, just in need of a little bit of repair'.

BIBLIOGRAPHY

Details of other, more specific, works will be found in the main text, particularly in the chapter on Continental heraldry (Chapter 6).

APPERT, G *Ancien Japon* (1988) [contains a section on *Daimyo* (the feudal nobility) and their *mon*]

BARKER, B *The Symbols of Sovereignty* [with a Foreword by J P Brooke-Little] (1979)

BARRON, Oswald 'Heraldry' in *Encyclopaedia Britannica*, 11th edn, 1910–11

BATY, Thomas (ed) *Vital Heraldry* [with an introduction by Julian Franklyn] (1962)

BENSON, A C, and ESHER, Viscount *The Letters of Queen Victoria – a Selection from Her Majesty's Correspondence between the years 1837 and 1861* 3 vols (1908)

BODLEY, John Edward Courtenay *The Coronation of Edward the Seventh – A chapter of European and Imperial History* (1903)

BRIGGS, G *Civic and Corporate Heraldry* (1971)

BROOKE, Christopher *The Saxon and Norman Kings* (1963)

BROOKE-LITTLE, J P *An Heraldic Alphabet* (1973)

— *Boutell's Heraldry Revised* (1978)

BRUNNER, H (compiler) *The Treasury in the Residenz Munich* (1971)

BURKE, John and John Bernard *Encyclopaedia of Heraldry, or General Armory of England, Scotland, and Ireland, comprising a registry of all armorial bearings from the earliest to the present time, including the late grants by the College of Arms* (1844)

Burke's Guide to the Royal Family (1973)

Burke's Royal Families of the World, Vol I (1977)

Burke's Royal Families of the World, Vol II (1980)

BUTE, John, Marquess of *Scottish Coronations* (1902)

COPINGER, W A *Heraldry Simplified* (1910)

DAVENPORT, C *The English Regalia* (1897)

Debrett's Coronation Guide (1911)

Debrett's Dictionary of the Coronation (1902)

EELES, F C *The English Coronation Service* (1902)

ELLIS, W S *The Antiquities of Heraldry* (1869)

ELVIN, C N *A Hand-book of Mottoes* (1860, reprinted 1963)

EMERY, W B *Archaic Egypt* (1961)

EVELYN, John *The Diary of John Evelyn, Esq., F.R.S. from 1641 to 1705–6. With Memoir, edited by William Bray, Esq., Fellow and Treasurer of the Society of Antiquaries of London*

FAIRBAIRN, *Crests of the Families of Great Britain and Ireland* (3rd edn, edited by Fox-Davies 1905)

FOGELMARCK, Stig (compiler) *The Treasury – The Regalia and Treasures of the Realm* [Sweden] (1970)

FOX-DAVIES, A C *A Complete Guide to Heraldry* (1909, revised edns 1949 and 1969)

— *The Book of Public Arms* (2nd edn 1915)

— *Heraldic Badges* (1907)

FRANKLIN, Charles A H *The Bearing of Coat-Armour by Ladies* (1923)

GALBREATH, D L *Papal Heraldry* (revised edn by Geoffrey Briggs 1972)

GARMONSWAY, G N (translator) *The Anglo-Saxon Chronicle* (1953)

GOODMAN, Jean (in collabration with Sir Iain Moncreiffe of that Ilk, Bt) *Debrett's Royal Scotland* (1983)

GRANT, F J *The Manual of Heraldry* (1st edn 1846, many subsequent editions)

GREECE, Prince Michael of *Crown Jewels of Britain and Europe* (1983)

GUILLIM, John *A Display of Heraldry* (1611; 6th edn edited by John Coats, 1724, is the best)

HALLS, Zillah *Coronation Costume and Accessories 1685–1953* (1973)

HESILRIGE, Arthur G M (ed) *Debrett's Heraldry* (1914)

HOLMES, M R 'The Crowns of England' in *Archaeologia*, Vol LXXXVI, 1936

— 'The Vanished Crown of Mary of Modena' in *The Illustrated London News*, 30 June 1956

HOLMES, Martin, and SITWELL, Maj-Gen H D W *The English Regalia – their History, Custody and Display* (1972)

HOWARD DE WALDEN, Lord (ed) *Some Feudal Lords and their Seals* (1903, reprinted 1984)

Illustrated London News, The (Coronation Souvenir editions, 1902, 1911, 1937, 1953)

INNES OF LEARNEY, Sir Thomas *Scots Heraldry* (2nd edn 1956)

JENKINS, Canon *Heraldry English & Foreign* (1886)

JOHNSTON, G Harvey *Scottish Heraldry Made Easy* (1912)

KEYNES, Simon, and LAPIDGE, Michael (translators) *Alfred the Great – Asser's Life of King Alfred and other contemporary sources* (1983)

LEGG, L G Wickham *English Coronation Records* (1901)

Liber Regalis (ed Lord Beauchamp) (1871)

LILIUOKALANI, Queen of Hawaii *Hawaii's Story by Hawaii's Queen* (1898, reprinted 1964)

LOUDA, Jiri *European Civic Coats of Arms* (ed Dermot Morrah FSA, Arundel Herald Extraordinary) (1966)

LYNCH-ROBINSON, Sir Christopher and Adrian *Intelligible Heraldry* (1946)

MACLEANE, D *The Great Solemnity of the Coronation* (1911)

MASSON, F *Le Sacré et le Couronnement de Napoléon* (1908)

MAUDE, Lt-Col G A *Letters from Russia 1856* (privately printed 1968)

METALLINOS, E *Imperial and Royal Coronations* (1902)

MONCREIFFE, Iain, and POTTINGER, Don *Simple Heraldry* (1953)

MURRAY, Rev Robert H *The King's Crowning* (1936)

NAYLER, SIR G *The Coronation of His Most Sacred Majesty King George the Fourth* (1839)

NISBET, Alexander *System of Heraldry* 2 vols (1916)

PANTER, Helen *King Edgar* (1971)

Papworth's Ordinary of British Armorials Reproduced from the original edition of 1874 (Introduction by G D Squibb QC BCL MA FSA JP, Norfolk Herald Extraordinary, and A R Wagner D Litt MA FSA, Richmond Herald) (1961)

PASSINGHAM, W J *A History of the Coronation* (nd, c1937)

PAUL, Sir J Balfour *Heraldry in Relation to Scottish History and Art* (1899)

PEPYS, Samuel *The Diary of Pepys* (ed with additions by Henry B Wheatley FSA) (1924)

PEREIRA, Harold B *The Colour of Chivalry* (1950)

PERKINS, Dr J *The Crowning of the Sovereign* (1937)

PERKINS, J H T *The Coronation Book* (1902)

PINCHES, J H and R V *The Royal Heraldry of England* (1974)

PLANCHÉ, J R (Somerset Herald) *The Pursuivant of Arms* (3rd edn 1874)

ROZEK, Michal *Polskie Koronacje i Korony* (1987)

SÄFSTRÖM, BO S *Uppsala Cathedral – A Guide* (1982)

ST JOHN HOPE, W H *Heraldry for Craftsmen and Designers* (1913)

SANDFORD, Francis *The History of the Coronation of James II* (1687)

SCHRAMM, P E *A History of the English Coronation* (1937)

— *Herrschaftszeichen und Staatssymbolik* 3 vols (1954–6)

SCOTT-GILES, C W (Fitzalan Pursuivant Extraordinary) *Civic Heraldry in England and Wales* (revised edn 1953)

— The Romance of Heraldry (revised edn 1965)

SELLWOOD, David The Coinage of Parthia (1980)

SETON, George The Law and Practice of Heraldry in Scotland (1863)

SITWELL, Maj-Gen H D W The Crown Jewels (1953)

SPERANSOV, N N Coats of Arms of Russian Principalities in XII–XIX Centuries (1974)

SQUIBB, G D The High Court of Chivalry (1959)

— The Law of Arms in England (2nd edn 1967)

STACPOOLE, W H The Coronation Regalia (1911)

STEVENSON, J H Heraldry in Scotland 2 vols (1914)

STEVENSON, Karen Artifacts of the Pomare Family (1981)

TWINING, Lord European Regalia (1967)

URQUHART, R M Scottish Burgh and County Heraldry (1973)

VOLBORTH, Carl-Alexander von The Art of Heraldry (1987)

— Heraldry, Customs, Rules and Styles (1981)

WAGNER, Sir Anthony Heraldry in England (1946)

— Heralds of England (1967)

— The Records and Collections of the College of Arms (1952)

WILLIAMSON, David
The Counts Bobrinskoy: A Genealogy (1962)

— Debrett's Kings and Queens of Britain (1986)

— Debrett's Kings and Queens of Europe (1988)

WOODCOCK, Thomas and ROBINSON, J M The Oxford Guide to Heraldry (1988)

WOODWARD, J, and BURNETT, G A Treatise on Heraldry, British and Foreign 2 vols (1892) [reprinted in 1 vol with new introduction by L G Pine 1971]

YOUNGHUSBAND, Sir G, and DAVENPORT, C The Crown Jewels of England (1919)

ACKNOWLEDGEMENTS

I wish to express my grateful thanks to all those who in various ways have helped me in the writing of this book. First, two members of the College of Arms, Sir Colin Cole, Garter King of Arms, for kindly writing a Foreword, and Patric Dickinson, Richmond Herald, for much good advice and encouragement. I also wish to thank Robert Yorke, archivist to the College of Arms, for his help in selecting some of the illustrations.

I am indebted to Derek Tooke for allowing me to use his arms as an example of how a coat of arms is designed.

Don Victor Franco de Baux, a widely acknowledged expert on all heraldic matters, has very kindly supplied me with all the material contained in the chapter on Continental heraldry and practice.

Brian North Lee has allowed me to use several items from his extensive collection of armorial bookplates as illustrations.

Others who have made valuable contributions are Arthur Addington, Juan Balansó, Robert Golden and Ted Rosvall.

Lastly, I must acknowledge with deep gratitude the help of my colleague John Verling, who has guided me safely through the intricacies of the word processor and averted many a near disaster.

DAVID WILLIAMSON

PICTURE CREDITS

Author page 56; author/Wappler, O W D 61; Bayerische Verwaltung der Staatlichen Schlösser, Munich 148–9; Central Press 89; College of Arms 2, 9, 15, 18–20, 37–40; Debrett's Peerage Ltd 35, 43 above; Fox Photos 87; Hawaii State Archives 115; HMSO 65 below, 66–72; ICI 16, 17; Kunthistorische Museum, Vienna 145 above; McPake, Gary 31; Murray, Peter 13; Museum of London 81, 90–1; National Museum of Budapest 112; National Museum of Warsaw 110 above; North Lee, Brian 25–9; Popperfoto 154; private collection 74; Residenz München, Schatzkammer 148–9; Restorian Workshop of Nidaros Cathedral 109; Royal Danish Collections at Rosenborg Palace 110 below, 111; Scotsman Publications Ltd 43 below; Tooke, Mr D A 49; the Treasury, the Royal Palace, Stockholm 102, 105–8; Württembergisches Landesmuseum, Stuttgart 145 below.

INDEX